IN PLAIN SIGHT

Anna Rashbrook

Cover design by: Cathy Walker

To Moira and Peter

My thanks to Dave, as ever, for being patient while I type away.

To Gweno for great proofreading

An enormous thank you to Sarah Jones, Theo Boiten, Lee Formistemporary Fletcher, Hilary Walker and Steve Malins for their support.

A massive thank you to my beta and arc readers; Larry, Christine, Dolly, Pat,Tanya, Trish, Louise, Judith, Marion, Debi, Corinne, Cathy and Jenny.

ALSO BY ANNA RASHBROOK

The Horses and Souls Series
Challenger
Compromise
Chaos
Christmas
Castles in the Air
Conclusion

The God, horses, and love Memoirs
Was it all about horses?
Finding
Horses and Heartbreak

Short Story anthologies
Collection
A Christmas Canter

Travel Memoirs
Dear Boot
Wish You Were Here - Holiday Memoirs Anthology
The Travel stories Collection (The
Travel Stories Series)

Supernatural Thriller
Tom

WW2 Racing mystery

In Plain Sight

Blogs
'So Where's the Snow?'
https://annarashbrook.wordpress.com

Anna's Horse Books
https://annarashbrook.wordpress.com

CONTENTS

LOOKING BACK

Whatever has happened in the past is always subject to memories, interpretations, and reactions. A writer can take events and twist and change them to his own will. And this is what I am doing now, using the past to create a new story that holds on to the truth as far as it can be recollected.

Things hidden at the time are now found, researched, and discussed. In the Second World War's aftermath, much remained unknown, and it needed time for information to be revealed. This wasn't deliberate, but just how things were communicated then. All the people here are long gone, so cannot ring me up and say, 'hey, it wasn't like that.' We each see what we want to. I am re-writing, but holding onto facts that cannot be changed.

This is a story based on truth, and I have researched it as well as I can to keep it truthful. I have immersed myself in that time, but it may well be my more modern language and ideology influence how I write. Yet love is the same. It never changes, does it? Now let's return to late 1944.

BEGINNING

December 1944

'Moira, it's time to get up. Now hurry up.'

Moira tugged both sheets and Nimbus the spaniel up over her head, a black hairy ear landing in her mouth. No, she couldn't pull the 'I haven't been to confession' excuse again. With a roar, she leapt out of bed and followed her mother down the stairs, Nimbus following the ruckus.

'Mother, I am putting my foot down, and you must listen to me.'

This stopped her bustling tracks. She turned to face Moira, that blank expression on her face. Mother was dressed in her business suit of calf length black skirt and jacket, which did nothing for her figure, white blouse, glasses and her hair set in ever rigid curls. She wasn't going to listen.

'I have had religion rammed down my throat since I was six years old when you sent me away to school,' Moira felt the bottled anger inside rising, but she thrust it down. 'I'm eighteen, old enough to leave school and I am making my choice not to go to Mass. It's all bells and smoke, I don't believe in it, and you're not sending another Jesuit priest to force his logic on me. I have a right to my opinion and I will keep it.'

All the time, her mother just looked, her lips moving as if words were trying to break out. But she said nothing, apart from an audible sniff as she slammed the front door. Wearily, Moira wandered into the kitchen and gave Nimbus his breakfast, which he greeted with joy. On the table stood a vaguely warm pot of tea and Moira was pouring herself a cup, when Father popped his head around the door.

'What did you say to your mother this time? The car door slamming gave it away.'

'I told her I wasn't going to Mass.'

'Oh, I see... I need to talk to you about something. Now, when you leave school next year, you can go to finishing school in Switzerland if you want.' He looked quizzically at her and grinned. 'The look on your face says you don't, just as I hoped. I'll break it to Mother for you, as that fits in with my plans. I want to buy Morton House in Kings Worthy and have an appointment at ten to have a look around. Would you like to come and see it with me?'

Moira needed no second bidding and quickly got ready. Father had one of the bright green vans with Croft and Sons emblazoned in gold on the side parked in front of the house. Mother, of course, had taken the larger, plain green van.

'I swopped some spuds for a gallon of petrol and this can go down as a delivery.' He smiled at her and slid onto the passenger side on the right.

'Excellent experience for your driving. Off you go, my dear.'

Moira slid onto the seat and, despite having to double declutch, they moved off with ease. The two grinned conspiratorially at each other. Alike in height and stature, both had a love for life, and an attitude that looked beyond convention. Dark haired Moira was her father's pet, but Mother had Peter, so that evened things out, didn't it? Mother knew nothing of these secret lessons. There was little traffic as they turned into the Worthy road, so they whooped with glee as they swept down the hill towards the village, narrowly missing a horse and cart.

'Take a left here dear, there's something that I think will interest you.' They turned into Headbourne Worthy and followed a lane. 'Look, here's a racing stables. Now won't that be fun to have that on your doorstep? You might be able to pop down on your bike and help with the horses.'

Moira said nothing, although something leapt inside her. Father really didn't know anything about horses, but saw her passion for them. Did he expect her to go and knock on the door and ask if she could ride the racehorses? She had heard of the trainer through the Racing Post, but he wasn't one of the more successful ones.

For Moira, it had all started with ponies, but after a couple of trips to point to points and the never forgotten day when they saw the legendary Brown Jack win the Queen Alexandra Stakes in

1934, her fascination with racing began. Moira even ran a racing syndicate at school for the few races that had been run during the war. So far, they had good winnings, and the nuns hadn't found out.

It suddenly dawned on her that she hadn't actually thought about what she would do after school. Moira had imagined not having to do boring lessons, staying in bed until she wanted, helping in the shop and, of course, riding. Surely racing would start again one day and maybe there would be chances for women to get into the profession? Before the war, there had been girls training for the examinations for the Institute of the Horse at Mrs Brown's riding stables, but they had seemed more like slaves and Moira had thought that wasn't for her. Now, this was something she would have to think and dream about. She would discuss it with her friends when she got back to school. Maybe Father's idea had been a good one after all. They passed the stables and drove into Kings Worthy, turning up Church lane. Father pointed to a lodge on the right and they turned with a bit of a screech up the little lane beside it and drew up in front of the house.

They stopped and looked through the windscreen, forgetting to get out. It was huge, built of a grey, yellowy brick, the imposing front door flanked by tall windows. Finally, they thought to jump out of the car, and just as they slammed the doors, a bright blue sports car rushed up the drive and skidded to a stop, spreading gravel. A tall, thin man peeled himself out, and Moira caught the glance he gave the van. It was a sneer of contempt. If it had been the old Bentley, now hidden in a garage on bricks, there would have been a nod of acknowledgment. His single-breasted blue suit had stiff creases and his tie looked so tight as if to strangle him. This was no war time economy suit. Where did he get the coupons? Typical chinless wonder. Moira caught the swift gesture of checking his slicked back hair, and forcing his face into professional indifference. Father, who was unaware of all this and probably wouldn't have cared if he had, grasped the man's hand.

'Mr Clayton, on time, as arranged. Let's get on and see around.' Father almost led the agent to the door and waited impatiently as the man struggled for the keys. Hah, not so clever now, thought Moira, and who was he, not to be serving in the forces? Wonder how he had got out of being called up?

Clayton might just as well not have been there as Moira and Father charged around the house, leaving his slick patter behind. The reception rooms were all sunny and looked onto the lawn, bordered by tall beech trees. Beyond that lay formal gardens, now fairly empty at the end of the season. They opened one of the tall glass doors, walked onto the lawn, and looked back at the house.

'What parties we will have here! And swing seats. Can you see Mother wheeling that tea trolley? We'll need some awnings over those windows for the hot weather…'

Father swept Clayton back into the main hall, who now at least made an effort, pointing out the good condition of the house and décor, and how much of the furniture was included in the sale. There was a ballroom, dining room, billiards room, and another smaller hall.

Through the baize door lay a large kitchen with two agas and an immense oak table. Off it lay the servants' hall, scullery, and various rooms, one of which seemed to be a gun room. Up the stairs behind them were a couple of plain servants' bedrooms. Moira, who was almost struck dumb at this, saw her dogs happily sleeping by the agas on cold winter days.

Returning to the main hall, they were swept up the main stairs by Clayton, who was trying to take control and shown seventeen bedrooms and five bathrooms. Well, that was what Father said later. Doors banged open and shut before they had a chance to look properly. Yet, Moira spotted one room looking over a red brick stable yard and demanded it for herself. Father agreed without argument. Out of the back door, they tore around a row of six looseboxes, garages, a kitchen garden, a rose garden, a tennis court, and an orchard right at the side of the house, two paddocks and another small house. Clayton's chatter diminished as the two effectively talked their way round. He might as well not have been there. But at last, there was no more to be seen, and they returned to the cars.

'Thank you so much, Mr Clayton. We've seen all that we need to for the moment. I will pop by your office and have a talk with your father in the next few days.' With another handshake, Father dismissed Clayton, who drove off with little to say.

'Obnoxious little tick. His father wangled him out of the forces. Asthma, what an excuse. I think the house will do us very nicely. All my friends can pop in for a drink. What fun we can have! That garden will support us, so we'll need a gardener... You could have a riding stables for all your chums.'

Moira put this stable comment to the back of her mind for later. 'But what about Mother? She would never be so far away from Winchester, the church and all her cronies with the Rotary Club and Inner Wheel and things like that.'

'Leave her to me. But just you think about it, we might have a butler, maids, cooks. Can't you see her lording it over her friends when they come to tea?' They both burst out laughing and drove home, making all sorts of plans, both sensible and ridiculous with the war time restrictions.

There was a fairly frosty reception when they got back late for lunch, but when the phone rang and it was Peter, Mother cheered up. She almost bounced into the room with the news that he was on his way home for a short leave. Since he had passed his course as a Lancaster Air Bomber, he had been posted to 106 Squadron in Lincolnshire, where he had been on training flights. Now all the crew were having long overdue leave. Father took the chance to talk to her about Morton House and as expected, when he appealed to her snobbishness, she almost agreed, subject to her own personal viewing and that they got servants. Moira's rebellion seemed forgotten, but there came a parting shot as Mother left for an Inner Wheel meeting.

'Rudy and Marga from the airbase will be here in an hour or so for their dictation. I'm sure you can do this, Moira, seeing as I won't be back...' she said in a no argument voice.

What could she do? The girls were stationed at Worthy Down Air Station, and through the church, had asked for help with their English. The trouble was, they would write phonetically in their own alphabet, which caused endless confusion and hilarity, but they felt it helped and were so grateful to have their chatter corrected over cups of tea. Later that afternoon, they were all sitting around the kitchen table.

'Rudy, you can't say that in English. Oh, how can I explain? You've just written something about what animals do in spring.' The three burst out laughing, but it was serious. Mistakes in communication cost lives, and the girls coming from Poland were very aware of the situation.

'I must tell you something, but don't pass

it on...' Rudy looked around her. She was always a bit on edge, but it was no secret she worked with MI6. 'I have to tell someone. Last night I had a phone call from my cousin, Jan. He's in the underground. All his family have been killed because they were Jewish.' The other girls took her hands as she began to cry. 'He told me that the battleship Gneisenau has left Kiel for Gdynia, so I passed it on to the RAF, and I hope they send a mission so all those on board die.' She became suddenly fierce and back in control, wiping her hands across her cheeks. There didn't seem to be any point in dictation, and the two took the next bus back to the station. The slight incident shook Moira, bringing it all home to her. The sequestered girls' boarding school blunted the edges of reality, but now some of the violence of war crept in.

Peter arrived early that evening, ever the stranger in his Air Force uniform. He puffed on the pipe he had arrived with in the summer, but this time Moira refrained from giggling. The childish bickering that had been their relationship up till now suddenly seemed irrelevant. It was better when they sat down to supper; he was dressed in a jumper and corduroys. She still saw him as her tall, annoying, blonde older brother. Now she suddenly perceived him as part of her family. He had Mother's eyes, was as tall as her, yet as easy going as Father. He was a contrast to the short gene Moira had caught from Father. From somewhere, Moira had black hair and hazel eyes. Mother said it was her Irish ancestry. Peter chatted about his fellow crew, some of the larks they had got up to and how boring waiting around for a mission could be. Moira vowed to send him more books.

There were a couple of days of peace in the house, as Peter was a real Catholic, enjoying Mass and going with Mother. Moira knew she would get the comparison talk again after he had gone, but Mother seemed happier with him at home. She even had a small get together for him to celebrate his upcoming 21st birthday as he probably wouldn't get leave again until the new year.

The usual crowd of her parents' friends arrived for the party, but the big surprise was the birthday cake. All the staff in the Jewry Street shop had clubbed together with coupons and ingredients, and the heavily iced cake was redolent of pre-war days. Moira saw how well Peter spoke the language of her parents as he chatted away. She became clueless at the 'how is school' question and only opened up if horses or dogs were mentioned. Not that she got more than a sip of the champagne.

Everyone toasted Peter with very small glasses, belted out the birthday song, and then clapped him for a speech.

'Well, thanks awfully for the party and the cake. It's such a different world here from the base and ops. Must say, it's been good to get a full night's sleep. And er, well, thank you all.' He clasped his pipe, and they cheered him again. Moira found her mother beside her, and herself being ordered to get packing, as tomorrow was time to return to school. It might only be an hour away on the train, but Farnborough Convent might be at the end of the world for all she cared. She hated the years of being sent away and couldn't wait for them to be over. Later, she was pulling the hated uniform out of the bottom of the wardrobe when a knock came at the door.

'Just thought I'd pop by and say thanks for those books you sent. Do enjoy a good detective novel. Back to that hell hole then?' Peter grinned at her.

Moira grimaced. 'I'll be out of there in July 45, and I can't wait. At least you enjoyed your time at Douai Abbey, it must have been a better school. Why didn't you drive down?'

'Well, I might have dented the car slightly. Don't tell the folks.' They smiled together. After years of bickering at last, there were some signs of friendship.

'Once you're free, you must come up to whatever base I'm on and meet the lads. Great bunch. Father said you've learnt to drive. Well done you, not to forget the double declutching.' Again, the hint of grown up friendship.

'I've been meaning to ask you. At the airfield next to school, there's the most strange planes. They sort of scream and they're terribly loud, go awfully fast too. No propellors. What are they?'

He answered in a pretend whispering voice. 'All a bit hush-hush, but they're called jets and they are the future. Don't tell anyone.' They giggled and not long after, he said good night. Moira dozed off, uniform still on the floor, this new treasure offsetting the dread of returning to school. Perhaps there wouldn't be any trains in the morning.

THE WEEK BEFORE CHRISTMAS, 1944

Once again, Moira threw her uniform into the wardrobe and shut the door firmly. This time for three glorious weeks, and after that, she would have only two more terms at school. Then it would be freedom. The school certificate wasn't a problem, after all, she would help with the family business, even if Peter ran it. Or she might get married. Or better, do something really exciting with horses. What was the point in subjects that you never used in life apart from a bit of writing, doing some accounts and drawing for fun? Only Mother and the school insisted that it was the most important thing in her life.

It would be Christmas a week today, and she had made presents for everyone that she hoped would be liked. Peter's would be posted to his base, and the others would be carefully wrapped in the brown paper she would sneak from Mary in the shop. She hurtled down the stairs and joined her parents for a game of cards with a gusto she hadn't felt for ages.

Breakfast the next morning was a treat with an egg and toast. Father was reading the paper and Mother fussing about some marks on the laundry.

When the doorbell rang, Father got up to answer it, as it was a good reason to escape the towels for a few minutes. He returned in a short while, looking ashen in the face and was silent. Mother looked up from examining the bills and her face drained, too. In his hand lay a small brown envelope. Father opened it rather than say anything else.

Deeply regret to inform you that your son F/O P. F. Croft missing from operations night 18/19th December. Letter follows pending receipt of written notification from Air-Ministry – No information should be given to the press

106 Squadron.

Father read it in a weak voice while Moira, and her mother listened in a shocked silence. Peter, the blonde sweetheart of the family, amiable, loving and becoming Moira's friend, was gone.

'Of course, he could be wounded. He may be a prisoner of war. We must all go and say a Mass for him.' Mother jumped up onto her feet, and as she searched for the car keys, Moira saw her hands shaking. For once, she didn't argue. Father, ever the chatterer, said nothing and came too, even though he was C of E. They said nothing on the journey and less on the way back, even while they had to wait for Mother telling the priest the news when they met at the church door.

Once home, Moira took to her bedroom and slammed the door owing to the weeping she heard coming from her parents' room. Father had taken the car and driven back into town. That night, he didn't return until well after closing time and was helped in by some of his Home Guard friends from the pub. He was so drunk he could barely stand. Moira helped him into a spare room as she knew Mother wouldn't stand for it, and as he crashed onto the bed, she wished she'd had a taste of that drink too.

After a sleepless night, imagining all sorts of distressing scenes with Huns and bombs and planes, she tried to see Peter hiding in a farm in Germany or even being bundled into a POW camp, but she didn't even know where he had been flying.

Over a silent breakfast when Mother said she wanted to ring the base, Father said in the most deadly and firm voice she must wait. He would say no more despite her beggings and for once she took note and obeyed him.

Over the next couple of days, the house retreated into silence. Father had been into the shop and told the staff and left his manager in charge. Then the letter arrived. He read it in a stone-cold voice that brooked no argument.

Dear Mr Croft,

I am writing to express my sympathy in the anxiety which must be yours upon receipt of the news that your son Flying Officer Peter Croft is missing from an overnight flight. I shall give you details also such details as I am able and could not be embodied in the necessarily brief and impersonal telegram.

On the night 18/19th December, 1944, my Squadron was detailed to bomb the important enemy Naval base of Gdynia and your son was the air bomber of one of the aircraft taking part. The raid was a success but I regret your son did not return. Nothing was heard from the aircraft after leaving base, and there is no definite knowledge of what happened, but it must be assumed that it was the victim of enemy ground defences or fighters. In either event , however, there is the possibility that the crew were able to 'bale out' and that, although prisoners of war, are quite safe. We all hope that this is indeed the case, and you may depend on the Red Cross obtaining all the information at the earliest possible moment.

Your son was a first class member of aircrew who had impressed me with his keenness and enthusiasm. He had a very sound technical knowledge and carried out his duties skilfully and with determination. I am most sorry to have lost him.

Once again, both personally and on behalf of all of the Squadron I offer my deepest sympathy and hope that there will be good news.

Yours sincerely
Wing Commander Commanding
No 106 Squadron, RAF

'So there is hope and I will never give up until I see his grave.' Mother said in a no arguing with me voice, but said no more. The silence was tearing Moira apart, and she got up and ran into the garden, not really knowing what to do, so she sat in the gazebo until she heard both cars leaving.

The next day was Christmas Eve, and Moira had to get out of the house and silence, so she walked into Winchester and the family shop. It was the biggest self-proclaimed green grocers and provision merchants in Winchester, with branches in Andover, Fareham and Gosport and had the enormous honour of being grocers to Winchester College. Over the door hung the banner, F. Croft and Sons, after her grandfather, but there would be no son to take over when her father died. It seemed ironic that it was still written in mosaic tiles on the front step, King & Co, the previous owners of the shop. Nothing seemed permanent anymore, and she gulped down the sadness. Immediately after Moira crossed the threshold, she was aware of an unsaid frisson that ran through the staff. There was much smiling and asking after school, but not the usual friendly banter.

They had the same decorations in the window that they had used since 1939, but done up this year with holly, ivy and anything green that could be found. Rationing and poor supply meant there was no longer the Christmas bounty of earlier years, with cakes, biscuits, special coffees, tins of exotic fruits, figs and Turkish delight, not to mention piles of winter vegetables and plump turkeys hanging by the meat counter. A few anaemic looking chickens lay on display. Still, the meat and cheese counters had more produce than on her last visit, and the scary bacon slicer had an enormous chunk ready to be cut beside it. The smell of freshly ground coffee streamed from the huge red grinder by the window. It permeated the entire shop and Moira found it a comfort. Mary, who was also her best friend among the staff, being not much older, came and stood beside her. Few customers were in the shop.

'Let's hope that next year all this will be over. I still can't believe that he hasn't been thrashed after D-Day. It all seems so long and we're all so tired. Fancy a cuppa?' Mary smiled.

The two slipped up the stairs through the household department smelling of disinfectant and new brooms to the dark back room filled with largely redundant tables used for packing orders. They raced up to the top floor, avoiding the office where Moira's father sat at his desk.

Kettle on, the pair sat at the long table and managed a natter about school and Mary's latest boyfriend, Ted. It was an entirely different world to Moira's cloistered life at the convent and she drank in all the tales about what Mary and her boyfriend had got up to on his last leave. Mary had great hopes for a ring the next time she saw him.

'Oh, heavens, I'm sorry. I'm being so tactless,' Mary said. Moira, for a split second, wondered what she was talking about, as for a few minutes the weight had lifted. She visibly slumped, but found herself engulfed in a hug that her stiff upper lip parents had never imagined she needed. Mary smelt of bacon, cigarettes and cheap perfume, but it calmed Moira, and she rested in it. Mary drew back and handed her a slightly soiled hanky.

'Now go on, let it all out. Our Mum says a good bawl is the world's greatest healer.' So Moira did. No other staff were about as this wasn't an official tea break time, so there wouldn't be any interruptions. The hanky wasn't sufficient, but a sleeve helped and the girls grinned at each other as Moira's eyes dried.

'Shame you can't come with us down the boozer tonight, it's going to be a right knees-up.' Moira knew as well as Mary that it wasn't going to happen, but the idea was appealing. They made the brew and chatted some more. Moira, feeling a little lifted, remembered to cadge some brown paper, and walked down the high street in a slightly better frame of mind. That was until Mrs Smithers caught her and engulfed Moira in a blast of gushing sympathy. Moira struggled away, knew she was right back to square one, and nearly returned to the shop and Mary.

Back in her bedroom, she wrapped her carefully made presents, but when she came to Peter's she didn't know what to do, he wouldn't need an embroidered book marker now. She ran down to the cellar and threw it in the boiler.

Christmas Day was probably the worst day in Moira's life, after having gone to Midnight Mass with Mother, like the lamb she should be. Moira prayed to a God she didn't believe in anymore, just in case he existed and could do something about all this. She imagined Peter receiving a Red Cross parcel in a POW camp, and that was better than a cold grave somewhere in Poland. Mother just dabbed at her eyes and said all the responses with fervour. None of them slept, and the early morning light found them sipping coffee in the sitting room, all glaring at the moth-eaten Christmas tree, laden with all the homemade decorations from the past few years.

'Perhaps next year, we'll have a new one. I'm sure the progress in Europe will have the Hun thwarted.' Father tried to be upbeat. 'Shall we open the presents now? Then we can have a nice fry up for breakfast. I shared the last of the bacon with the staff, but I got some for us.'

So they did, with Moira's parents being suitably, if not overly pleased with their pipe holder and doilies for the table. Moira quite liked the books on horses, but didn't want to appear effusive.

'Did you get something for Peter?' Mother suddenly asked in a sharp tone.

'I did, but as he won't need it, I put it in the boiler…' She had to speak the truth. Mother sniffed. 'What was it? We could have given it to a charity.'

'No, it was for him and no one else,' Moira almost shouted. 'It's not as if he hasn't been here for Christmas in the past. He was in Canada the year before last. Don't be nasty, Mother.'

Then came that closing down look, and she went off to cook.

'Let's try to get through today without any upset?' Father almost pleaded. She had never seen him without that glint of humour in his eyes, so Moira buttoned up the stiff upper lip and played the dutiful daughter for the rest of the day.

They ate the dry chicken, and pudding bulked out with carrots and breadcrumbs, saying it tasted as good as any other Christmas lunch. They talked about good Christmases of the past, trying to infuse into the day the spirit of those times, even speaking of Peter, as if he was in Canada, not the spectre sitting at the end of the table. But as they spoke, their hearts inside were frozen.

They weren't alone. Families all over the country faced the same thing. It wasn't just grief, but a national weariness, born of trying times, lack of sleep, the threat of bombing raids, stress and sheer misery. Of life becoming such a struggle, even in the simple things like buying food. The country lay under a blanket of exhaustion, heartbreak and the strain of putting a brave face on it all the time. The day left Moira with a hatred of Christmas and her heart only warmed slightly when she returned to school and some sense in the cloistered life that had become her normality.

FEBRUARY 1945

'No, I won't do it.'

'Please, Moira, we just can't face it. Your mother has high blood pressure and the strain would be too much and I've so much on with the shops.' Father tried to smile through the exaggeration.

'Why can't you get a van to collect the stuff? Surely most people get their things sent to them?' she wailed. Never in her life had her parents been united. There had always been one of them set against the other, someone on her side. She had barely got through the front door for half term, and now this.

'I don't know why they won't send his things. It is unusual. Maybe it's just the state of the war.' Father looked weary, and Moira gave in, but not without a great resentment. Why demand this from her? Wasn't she grieving too?

'So how am I physically going to carry all of this? I saw his trunk, and there must be suitcases. And what about his car?'

Clearly, her parents hadn't considered all the ramifications.

'The trunk will fit in the car,' Mother said firmly.

'So now you're expecting me to drive hundreds of miles? It's not as if I've been able to take a test.' Moira searched for excuses.

'No, there's another way,' Father came in. 'You will take the train and then a taxi to the airbase. It will then take you back to the railway station and you will send it all in the luggage van, even the car. I will meet you at Winchester station.'

It seemed there was no way out, and on a bleak morning, Moira stood on Winchester train station, with a meticulously planned timetable in her hand. Father had worked it all out, even ringing stations along the line to check for problems. But wartime trains had a mind and agenda of their own, stopping and starting and missing stops on a whim. She had no great faith that she could do the trip in a day and hoped that she would be able to find somewhere to stay if she got stranded overnight.

She travelled on train after train to Lincoln, change after change, and missed connections. Yet, she arrived in the afternoon's gloom, into the wilds of flattest Lincolnshire. It was what she imagined the tundra to be like, with bitter winds crossing farmlands and marshes, cold, flat and inhospitable. It was such a contrast to the mild south coast and somehow also comforting, matching her inner feelings and frozen heart.

Because of the air base, a taxi wasn't too difficult to find, especially when she told the driver he would have to wait.

At the gates, she handed over her letter and they drove in. They parked by the Mess and she got out and stretched. A tall officer came out to meet her.

'Miss Croft? It's so good of you to do this.' The rest of his sentence blew away by the noise of a flight of Lancasters coming in to land. Moira stood and watched in silence, forgetting everything around her. The roar of the engines and the sheer size of the planes were terrifyingly awesome. Why did they come home and not Peter? Where was he?

As the engines stopped, she turned. 'Did you know my brother? Where is his car?' Possibly it had been repaired.

'No, I'm afraid not in answer to both of your questions, but there'll be some chaps in the mess who can. Why don't you pop in over there, and sign, load up the stuff and I'll dig these chaps out. Can't ask you in, rules you know...'

Moira signed for the familiar trunk, a suitcase, and a bound cardboard box. She lugged the smallest, and the clerk helped with the heavier ones and put them in the taxi. He knew where the car was.

'He pranged it, good and proper, a while ago. It's under a tarpaulin, round the back, it will cost more than a few bob to mend, if it's possible. Amazing what a pint, a puddle, and a brick wall can do...'

Suddenly Moira grew angry with the world, Peter for leaving her to have to explain this to her parents, her parents for giving her this job to do. She didn't want any bonhomie from so-called friends. She didn't want happy anecdotes. They would just increase the pain. Each of these uniformed men could be and might be Peter, she didn't want to know them. It would feel better standing in the bitter cold than trying to be friends.

The enormity of war hit her as never before. The hurt and cold seemed to crystallise within her, manifesting as an anger that gave an edge to her natural sparkle. She couldn't see that unforgiveness would eat her heart into a bitter core if she didn't let some sort of healing in. A few minutes later, the taxi sped back to the station.

It was nearly midnight when she got back to Winchester, but Father waited for her outside the station. He and a porter put everything in the van's boot and they drove home in silence. To Moira's surprise, Father didn't go to unload it.

'But what will you do with it? Surely Mother will want to go through his things?'

'We're not able to face that yet. I'll just take the documents and his keys. We might never be ready, but we wanted him home. And that will be Morton House. I'll drive it over there in the morning, and we'll store it in the loft until we can face things.'

Moira was astounded. All that to put it in the loft? Why couldn't they have left it at the base? This was all too much to take in. Tomorrow she was going riding and would each day for the rest of half term. Mother couldn't dare moan at the cost, nor Father the petrol.

EASTER 1945

As the news seemed more and more hopeful, and the weather warmed after the cold start to the year, it was as if the end of the war was changing the very world. No one knew who would survive and who would come home. The uncertainty brought with it hope, a raising of spirits and, at the same time, despair.

Moira leapt from the train, feeling happier than for a long time. Another girl at school had lost family and that had been a balm as they shared stories. And it helped that she wasn't returning to Holmcote and all the memories. Her parents had moved into Morton House, and she looked forward eagerly to her new home.

Father waited outside the station with the green delivery van, but it made it easy to throw all her stuff in the back and them to roar up to Kings Worthy. As they turned in the drive, she saw fresh curtains hanging at the gate lodge.

'A Mr and Mrs Gill live there, they used to work for the Duke of Beaufort.' He threw a triumphant grin at Moira. 'There's Laurence, the gardener. He lives in the cottage at the back. What do you think? Your mother is so pleased with me. She's busily arranging the sitting room at present, so maybe leave her be.' That old hint of humour was back in his manner, although not as strong as before.

'How did you find all these people?' Moira was astonished. Even she had realised that there were few people in service during the war and there would be a shortage afterwards. Her friends at school had complained about being made to do housework.

Father tapped the side of his nose. 'When one is in the trade, one has contacts.' He would never be drawn for more details.

They swerved onto the gravel at the house entrance, spreading stones all over the place. With a flourish, Father got out, and like a chauffeur, opened the door for Moira. With the eagerness of a boy, he bounced into the house with her bags.

In a short time, cleaning, more furniture and being used had transformed the air of the house. No longer unloved, it was awakening. Furniture and carpets had been cleaned and looked alive as their colours came through as the dust lifted. Even one of Mother's classic flower arrangements gave an air of love and greeting.

He led Moira up the sweeping stairs to the room she had asked for. All her things were there in boxes, and a bookcase for all her horse and dog books stood in the corner. The bed was made up, and the curtains blew in the breeze from an open window. She looked out at the stable yard below. There were loose boxes just waiting for chestnut, bay and grey heads to be looking over them. Ideas and plans she had concocted with her horsey pals might now be possible.

'Now, you can't have all the stables. I want one to grow mushrooms in, so we will need the fertiliser. I got the idea from the gardener I talked to the other night down at the pub. I'm also going to breed my rabbits. There was never enough room before. With the garden, we moved in at just the right time of year. We can be self -sufficient in fruit and veg, and I'm going to teach you to shoot. There's plenty of game about with the gamekeepers away fighting. Now chuck your bags and let's get some tea.'

It was almost unreal to Moira as she ran down into the main sitting room, where her mother stood judging the angle of the picture of the lady in blue above the fireplace. It was her favourite.

'Ah, Moira, good you're home. What do you think of this place now? Haven't I transformed it?'

Moira didn't argue, 'It's wonderful, Mother, it's going to be smashing living here.' She had seen the pictures of Peter on the wall by her mother's armchair and didn't want to spoil anything. Then came a clattering and rolling of wheels and an elderly lady pushed the enormous tea trolley into the room. She looked just like a grandmother should do, with her grey hair swept into a bun, her cheeks rosy. She wore a slightly grubby apron, so when Moira caught her mother's glance at it, she stepped in.

'Hello Mrs Gill, I'm Moira.'

'Guessed that,' she grinned. 'Now, can you give us a hand with this teapot?'

Tea passed uneventfully with talk of school, her report, which for once had been ok, little tales of things that happened in the move and quite a lot about when Mother would host the Rotary Club for dinner.

'Now, my dear, why don't you have a real explore.' Father was giving her some freedom. He knew she was itching to get outside before Mother demanded something and Moira was off.

She changed into her old jodhpurs and blouse. So what if there were no horses? These were the most comfortable things to wear. At her leisure, she checked the paddocks, and the fences and gates seemed sound. She looked into the looseboxes, all in tiptop condition, clean with the mangers scrubbed. The tack room just ached for leather, rugs and a groom sipping tea by the fire, with a beagle warming himself with him. She sighed and looked in at the walled garden. It had already been dug over and lines of green leaves ran along the beds.

'Now, don't go walking on my nice fresh beds.' Moira jumped out of her skin to find a man in a cloth cap and jacket grinning at her.

'Hello, Mr Laurence, I wouldn't dream of it.'

'I'm certain, Miss Moira, and when we need some help picking things, I'm sure you'll help.

Come and look at this greenhouse.' It was clearly his pride and joy.

'Grapes, peaches, strawberries, you name it, we'll be able to grow them. Just make sure you check with me before you pick.'

'I will, and it looks wonderful. You must have worked so hard in here. When we looked at the house, it looked sad and unloved.'

She had said the right thing as he smiled. 'Well, I've got a bit of help from a lad from the village, and I'm ticking over nicely. Now where's he gone? He was supposed to be cleaning out some cold frames…'

Moira escaped, making her way back into the house through the kitchen door. She was engulfed in the smell of a roast cooking, the like of which she barely remembered. The enormous table had been scrubbed, and Mrs Gill rolled pastry in a cloud of flour.

'Pour us a cuppa and sit down, my dear, and tell me all about yourself.' And Moira found herself doing just that, all about school, her friends, riding the horses she liked at the stables, her books and her plans. Then Mrs Gill asked a tough question.

'And your brother, did you and he get on?' The question so disarmed Moira from the usual sympathetic remarks that she opened up, finding it suddenly easy and even a relief to talk to a kindly, distanced person. By the end, a little of that dead weight within her lifted for a while. She was just running out of things to say, having just talked about him as a brother, not what happened, when the door swung open and a tall man walked in, carrying a gigantic box of fruit and vegetables.

'These are all ends from the shop and we must use them up.' He could have been nothing except a butler; thin, with a long, noble face. He looked down at Moira and smiled. 'Miss Moira, so glad to meet you.' Gill plonked the box down and looked at his watch. 'Your mother requested dinner at seven?' Moira looked at hers with horror and, with a wave to them, rushed upstairs to tidy herself up.

When she entered the dining room, it was a bit awe-inspiring. Only one long table with only three places laid, and a large sideboard were in there. It was a relief that the room looked out over the garden. It made what was a quite sombre room lighter. Who on earth had thought that a dark red was a good colour for such a room?

'Moira, jodhs might be okay for running around, but not for meal times. Please make yourself presentable,' Mother ordered. Moira obeyed, resisting the argument that it was just the three of them. Something of the grandeur of the place made her feel that she should be of the same quality.

When she came down again, they began on the now tepid soup. Then came a roast that Moira hadn't seen the like of for many years. Yes, many of the vegetables may have come in the box, but there were also Yorkshire puddings, roast potatoes and a rich gravy, even if the wafer -thin sliced beef was a small serving. Mother had never been the best cook. How the Duke of Beaufort must miss Mrs Gill now, Moira mused. The crumble that followed filled her inside like no meal had done — well, forever.

'We certainly have found a treasure in Mrs Gill.' Mother echoed Moira's thoughts. 'Now we have things we must discuss.' Moira saw Father looking out the window.

'When you leave school, you will naturally return here to live. We all think that the war will be over soon, and we will have to think of your future. Of course, we hope you will find a nice young man and settle down, but until then, you will help with the house, the shops and, of course, when I need you to help with social events.'

Oh, no, not the Inner Wheel. It was unlike Mother to be so positive.

'You might, of course, find some suitable job, maybe do some typing. But your place is with us here. Now I can't say fairer than that, can I?' Mother nearly smiled.

'I always imagined I would help with the business...' At last, Moira found the courage to broach the subject that they were all avoiding. 'But you've not said anything. Is there any news from the Red Cross?' Moira asked.

Her parents shook their heads, and for a couple of seconds, remained silent.

'Of course, I will be here in any way you need

me. I will simply be glad to be at home with you.' Perhaps she should go into diplomacy. Her parents looked slightly cheered. Moira knew she was the second choice and their pain was too raw, even now.

'As you will soon be grown up, we expect you to manage yourself,' Mother continued. 'When you run a household, all of these things are necessary. Mrs Gill will teach you a lot. But you must be presentable. When you come home, you will receive a monthly allowance for clothes and any other things. Extras, of course, we will discuss. And of course, as you can drive, you may use the cars. We hope this will be a happy place for us.' Mother's speech ended.

'Will I be allowed to have another dog now, and possibly a horse?' She was unable to resist it and saw the badly hidden grin on Father's face.

'We shall see,' Mother said stiffly and rose, discussion closed.

'Just wait until you come home,' Father grinned broadly. 'Now, let's listen to the news. Things are moving on so fast.'

Indeed, it seemed there was light at the end of the tunnel. The next day, Father decided that if things were going to change, it was time to do a stock take at the shop. Moira found herself bundled into coveralls and made to knuckle down with the sheer tedium of checking what was and wasn't on the shelves and in storerooms. Yet it was fun, as the staff treated her as one of them, and Moira had many giggles and secret fag breaks with Mary when Father was diverted. Moira did this with a willingness, as at times she saw a touch of sadness when he thought no one was looking. Peter had helped sometimes in the shop and they remembered him with affection. Perhaps Moira wouldn't have to be forced into marriage and the many grandchildren that her mother clearly wanted. She could grow into and take over the business. Filled with a new sense of purpose on returning to school, Moira actually made some effort with her work, as the dreaded school certificate was looming on the horizon.

JULY 1945

As Moira woke, the words from H. G. Wells' *Mr Hoopdriver* leapt into her head, 'The exquisite sensations of the First Holiday Morning… which is the most glorious, for you hold your entire fortune in your hands.'

And today, the spectre of having to return to school was banished forever. Certificate passed, it was over, finished, life was full and ahead of her, freedom called. That it was a beautiful day helped too. The end of the war was the icing on the cake. Not that it had yet made a tremendous difference. Rationing continued, but petrol was slowly coming back on the market, or so Father said, and there were no more dreary blackouts on the houses. People were different too, especially after the parties on VE day. Not that the nuns at the Convent had let them do much except play a little music, and of course, go to Mass. That night, London sounded amazing on the radio, and the newspapers had such incredible photos of people in the crowds. This missing out was a minor blemish on perfection. Father said there were things being organised in the village, so there would be some fun.

People looked forward to family coming

home, although the war in Japan was going on. Mother last night had that steely look on her face, saying she was now going to get on to all the various government departments to find out what had happened to Peter, as there lay a spark of hope that he would be found alive in Europe somewhere. Father said nothing to the outburst.

Best of all had been that Moira now had a bank account, and the promised monthly allowance. She was tempted to throw the old uniform on the bonfire in the back garden, but Mother bundled it all away to be cleaned and sent to the school for scholarship girls. Whatever its fate, she would never have to see it again.

From somewhere in the house, a gong rang. This was a new thing, and it seemed an extravagance after the austerity of the war. Breakfast wasn't a feast in the dining room, but she was allowed two eggs, as there were now chickens and ducks in runs by the walled garden.

'Now, what will you be doing today?' asked Mother.

'I would rather like to go into Winchester and look for some new clothes and things.'

'That sounds sensible. You can go with your Father and be back for lunch. Now remember this money will have to last you all month and you will need some suitable clothes for evening and entertaining. Perhaps I should come with you after all.'

'No, Mother, I'm sure you won't need to.

Hodders, and Sherriff and Ward will be able to advise me,' Moira smiled brightly.

'Hmm, and don't forget your coupons. You can only buy so much.'

'It shouldn't be a problem, Mother. I've been saving them up.' Disaster averted, Moira and Father got away before she could change her mind.

'Now, this afternoon, I need to take you to meet some people. Nothing scary, but it will be such fun.' He wouldn't be drawn any more.

Feeling like a woman about town, Moira took herself to the largest department shop in Winchester, Sherriff and Ward, found an assistant about her age and explained she needed things for evenings and guests. She found two dresses, a cardigan, and some plain underwear in the sales, and came away with some new shoes that would do for all occasions. But this wasn't her major mission. She then took herself up to Wilds, the sports shop, and riding outfitters. After new boots, breeches and jodhpurs, a jacket and a bowler, there was precious little left of her allowance and she had to make some promises about the coupons. But her father's name was good with all the businesses in Winchester, and she knew it wouldn't be a problem. She just made it back to the shop in Jewry Street before Father left. Once home, she rushed upstairs, put one of the dresses on and ran down to lunch. Mother didn't look impressed, and demanded a complete account of what she had bought.

Then the argument started.

'You are not going to act like a tomboy any more, Moira. You cannot live in jodhpurs. You are a young woman of good class and you will have to meet many other girls in the same order. I will not have you lacking. I see I must take you shopping, so you are suitably dressed for your station in life. There are many wealthy Catholic families in the area. You won't find a suitable husband going around in trousers or riding gear. It's just not on.' She was getting redder and redder in the face, Moira imagined her glasses steaming up.

'I think you may find, Mother, that many of the wealthier families ride, and that this will be an important accomplishment if she is to mix with society. After all, that Sussex family you keep going on about, all hunt, and keep a stable of thoroughbreds,' stated Father firmly.

How on earth did Father know all this? But once again, he had saved the day and the two of them exited as fast as possible after pudding. Moira knew she wasn't going to escape Mother's attempts at gentrifying her. There would be more battles ahead.

'Now pop on those old jodhpurs you have. I don't want you looking like something from Moss Bros,' Father smiled. In comfortable old clothes, Moira jumped in the van.

'Where are we going, Father, and thanks for rescuing me.'

'Not far.' He wasn't going to be drawn.

He drove through the quiet roads and Moira recognised the lane where the racing stables lay. To her joy, they swung through the huge wooden gates and drew to a halt on a patch of gravel in front of some brick and flint buildings. It was the stable yard of the trainer, Tommy Rayson. Moira was enthralled to be actually visiting a real racing stables, and looked around with great interest.

On three sides stood blocks of brick and flint stables, with green painted doors. In between them lay a large area of mown grass. Not a scrap of hay was blowing around, unlike the stable in Winchester where Moira had learnt to ride. To their left was a vast manor house, built of the same, with a slate roof and mullioned windows. Around it lay a formal flower garden and lawn. Beyond this, Moira saw barns, outbuildings and paddocks lay all around the property. She sighed, this was just wonderful.

Out of the house came a tall man, plump, with thinning grey hair, and the most dirty, scruffy corduroy trousers Moira had ever seen.

'Harold, hello. I guess this is your daughter?' Moira found her hand engulfed in a firm grip and she was appraised by searching blue eyes.

'All during the war, I used this mare to go about the place in a dogcart. Now the petrol is coming back in the garages, I don't really need her here eating her head off. Your father says you've ridden at Mrs Brown's school in Winchester, so you should be of a reasonable standard, but I think we must pop you up first.'

Moira realised she was like a goldfish with her mouth hanging open, so she snapped it shut and nodded.

'Brian, bring the mare to the near paddock.'

One of the stable lads, who had been darting across the yard, turned back and went into the furthest block. Moira now saw the internal looseboxes and heard a door being swung open.

Brian appeared with a small bay mare of about 14 hands high, hogged with a ragged white blaze between her eyes. She seemed feisty, swinging out, as if in a hurry. The lad stood her still and checked her girth.

'Go ahead,' Tommy laughed. Moira was without an apple, but the mare sniffed her hand and seemed friendly enough.

'Leg up?' asked Brian. Now, Moira was no taller than her father, so the mare seemed a good size to her, but she wasn't going to be seen as a beginner. However, before she could get hold of the stirrup iron to mount, she found herself legged up. It was most odd, but really convenient. She swiftly adjusted her stirrups and got ready to go. Brian gave her a wink and pointed to the paddock. The two men were already making their way down to open the gate.

The mare strutted down the yard, and she looked around her with great interest. Moira's spirit rose. This was a real horse, not a tired riding school pony, and they would have fun together.

Once on the beaten track in the paddock, Moira wasted no time in getting to know her mount. She felt a little strong, giving a powerful tug on the reins when Moira asked for canter. She took off, but there was a lively cheerfulness about her, and she soon came back under control. From the fence, Tommy pointed over to some small training hurdles. With great glee, the two turned themselves and scuttled over, the mare even putting in a buck after the last one. Moira laughed out loud and made the mare walk to the fence. She wasn't blown or hot, just full of joy.

'Looks like you two will get on,' said Tommy with a grin. 'She's not everybody's cup of tea, and has her moments. You might like to come and ride out for me sometime too, though you will need to get those stirrups up and ride like a jockey.' Moira was thrilled. Things were getting better and better. Could this be the chance she had been dreaming of? What else could she say but, 'I'd love to!'

'Well, you get that mare settled in, yourself used to her, and then pop down and we'll sort you out. I often need extras in the mornings.' Tommy opened the gate, and Moira rode back to the yard.

'Where do I put her?'

'You're riding her home,' Father laughed. 'She can go out in the orchard paddock. Laurence has filled the trough and checked the fence.'

'Oh, Tommy,' Moira knew she was breaking convention by not calling him Mr, but he seemed like Father, one who wouldn't be bound by daft rules.

'What's her name?'

'Star.' He waved goodbye and Moira rode out of the gate. The mare strode along looking around her again with great interest, even trying a shy at a child running around in a garden. It didn't worry Moira. She had dreamed of such a thing through her childhood and it was finally coming true. The mare's name didn't seem right; the mark was more of a splash than a star. Then she remembered a novel she had loved that was all the rage, 'Forever Amber', scandalous in content, all about the affairs of a cheeky courtesan. The girls at school had passed it around and devoured it eagerly away from the gaze of the nuns who had heard enough of it to know it shouldn't be read by genteel young ladies. This mare was of the same bouncy, cheerful disposition and would surely be trouble at times. What could she be, but Amber?

It was glorious riding up the drive. Nimbus came rushing out, barking at the new sound, but quietened when Moira shouted. He followed her to the gate. When he got too close, Amber aimed a hoof at him and they made a truce. He would keep clear. Moira dismounted and took the saddle off, putting it on the fence. She realised there were a lot of things missing. She didn't even have a head collar or a brush. Amber didn't care, catching her against the railings so she could have a good scratch. Moira pushed her away and led her into the paddock, where there was high, lush grass.

Slipping the bridle off, not catching Amber's teeth, she let her go free. With a snort, she trotted off, stopped and with a grunt, fell to the ground and had a serious roll. Heaving herself up, her head went to the grass and the sound of munching filled the air.

'Nice bit of manure now for me beds.' Moira jumped out of her skin. It was Laurence. 'I'll get that young scamp to come and clear it, so you'll have a nice clean field and us great veggies. Your father is in the yard. He needs a hand.'

Mystified, Moira went round. Her father was heaving a bag out of the back of the van.

'Tommy has sent you some grooming stuff, halter and things, pop those in the tack room. Then come and see what I've got.'

In the van were boxes in which sat six large white rabbits. 'Laurence and I have built some hutches, help me carry them around the back. We'll breed them and with my four does have loads of cheap meat that's not on the ration. I don't think I can shoot enough of them for the pot. Tommy put me on to this man down the road...'

The rabbits seemed happy in their hutches, there was already hay and greens for them. Only the buck was on his own, as the does should already be pregnant, then afterward the births, his services would be needed.

'I'll pop down the lane and pick weeds for them,' Father grinned.

'Moira. Harold.'

An imperious call came from the house, so the two, putting their joys aside, went to find out what the mistress required.

'We have people for drinks in an hour, and look at the state of you two. Go and get changed. There are some sandwiches in the sitting room for afterwards. Moira put on the blue dress. It's the better of the two.'

They obeyed, Father whispering conspiratorially that while he had mentioned the horse, he hadn't said anything about the rabbits.

The evening was Moira's introduction into the adult world. Three couples arrived, all cronies of her mother, but also possible business contacts for the shops, so Father was on his best form. Moira found herself being given trays of delicious looking canapes to hand around and wondered again how Mrs Gill found the means to do it. Moira now got some attention, visible as the only child, yet an official woman, having left school. It meant she could sneak several sherries and even smoke a cigarette. No doubt Mother would have something to say later. No one mentioned Peter.

The people, whose names Moira never remembered, all asked the same questions: how was school, what are you going to do this summer? We must have some tennis parties. Then onto their own perfect children. Moira was on the point of saying she was going to be a nun when some fresh faces arrived. It was Tommy and a younger man who must be his son, as the two looked so alike. The son didn't look much older than her, so she wasn't alone, which came as a huge relief. Father went straight over and began the introductions, even to Mother, who put on her polite face.

Moira found herself with the Tommy look alike. He had the same startling blue eyes as his father, taller than Moira only by a little, lean with a full set of dark, bushy hair, but thankfully no baggy trousers. 'How do you do? I'm Moira,' she stammered.

'Yes, I know,' he gave her a big grin. 'You impressed Tommy with your riding. That mare can be really difficult. I'm Monty.'

'Oh, of course,' Moira was embarrassed. 'Do you work with Tommy on the yard?' Heavens, what do you say to people?

'Not all the time. I'm a National hunt jockey, steeplechases, hurdles and that sort of thing. I'm on my summer break until the season kicks off again in the autumn. We'll soon be getting the horses up from grass to get them fit. I grew too tall for flat racing and spent the war flying a desk because I have poor eyesight. But that was a blast, as I got a few races in as so many other jockeys were away fighting. I'm just getting my trainer's licence too.'

'Have you ridden in the Grand National?' As she said it, she bit her words. The race hadn't been run since 1940. 'Oh, that makes me sound so stupid.'

They both laughed. 'I saw Brown Jack's last win. It was amazing.' She tried to make amends.

'We were at the meeting, too. It wasn't long after my mother died.'

'I'm sorry.' Moira hoped she looked sympathetic.

'No, please don't. She had been ill for a long time.'

Moira was out of her depth, and for once in her life, stuck for words. Nimbus saved her. He had found a way in and was checking the floor for any crumbs.

'Oh no. I'm going to be in more trouble. I need to get him out before Mother sees him.' She grabbed Nimbus's collar and dragged him out one of the French windows. Outside, she found Monty had followed her.

'I can't stand that sort of thing. Thanks for getting me out,' he said. Moira, having already perceived she would soon think the same thing, agreed.

'Come and see Amber in her new home.' The two wandered off to the paddock, Nimbus joyfully running with them as Moira explained the new name.

She'll explode on all that grass. You need to take the top off it, was Monty's unexpected observation of the mare eating as fast as a horse could.

'How do you mean?' Moira was surprised.

'If you get one of your men with a scythe to

cut the grass to about six inches, it will be fine.'

'I'll talk to Father, but she'll be ok tonight, won't she? Come and see the new rabbits.' He nodded, and they wandered around the place with inconsequential chatter. Then, to a mutual relief, a rather loud owl hooted.

'That's Tommy,' Monty grinned. 'I guess we'll meet to ride out one morning?'

'I think I might have a lot to learn.'

He smiled. 'You can always join us on er, Amber, to see what goes on. Meet us any morning on the lane up to the old racecourse gallops. We usually leave the yard by 7.30.' He waved and disappeared.

Back inside, most of the guests had also departed, and Gill was clearing up the debris with her mother supervising.

'Well, I suppose your behaviour was passable, but that dog must be locked up when we have visitors.' Was there never a good word from her?

'Now, tomorrow morning we are going to a flower arranging demonstration, so you can have a go. I don't want to do them all the time.' So what did she do with her time?

'Those frocks you bought are just not right, we'll get some better ones. Then we must see about an evening gown and some evening informal wear for you. They will have to be made. We'll go to that nice little lady in Parchment Street.'

To Moira's fury the next morning, as not only couldn't she ride and meet the racehorses,

Mother's plan included Mass before the flowers. Moria was propelled to the front pew and blocked her ears to the droning on in Latin. She bobbed up and down as expected, and had a minor rebellion by not genuflecting or taking communion. Mother needed to push past to get her wafer.

In the few moments Mother was away, Moira had a moment of pain. If only Peter was there, he had no problem with the bells and smoke. He never saw the need to question all around him. In the quietness, she felt that grief return, too. The lack of news was the worst thing. Maybe if it was settled one way or the other, they could have a memorial and the grief would go. The anger she had felt at being duped that morning, now, somehow, got mixed up with that core of ice within her. She almost shivered. No, as the news was coming out from all over Europe of concentration camps, mass graves and destroyed towns, she realised this hate of all the Germans professed to must be held on to and remembered, otherwise it would all eventually happen again.

Yet, knowing she had to get through the morning with her mother, she battened it down and put on the stiff upper lip. One didn't show one's feelings, it wasn't done. Her family was never a hugging type, and she was now glad, as it helped to control her feelings. Just some news, one way or another, please.

The Guildhall was filled with women in their best, and not a few girls about Moira's age. They all appeared to be eager to find out how to twist flowers into containers in many shapes, and were enthralled at an enormous display by Constance Spry in the foyer. Moira wondered how many people would actually have room for such a small shrubbery in their parlour. To her dismay, after the woman talked about moss for the flowers to go in, types of vases, everyone was directed to a table covered in flowers, lumps of green vegetation and vases of all sizes. Now they needed to prove they had listened, and at the same time, get hints and tips.

Moira found herself by a tall, bespectacled girl who grinned at her. 'Isn't this such fun? I'll go home and make our house so wonderful. I've even been helping the gardener grow some lovely flowers for the house.' Moira saw Laurence's face if she offered to help and was relieved. She let the girl rabbit on and hoped she wore a pleasant expression on her face. A clap of hands from the front came with a command that they were to begin.

Moira grabbed the first vase she could reach, and some green feathery moss, which she jammed in the vase. It was soaking wet and dripped all down her new dress. Others looked at their flowers, holding them up to the light, comparing them to each other. Moira copied them, then after a while jammed them all in the vase, too. It seemed to work as they fell out in a natural arch, with the tallest at the top. Hah, take that, Constance Spry she laughed to herself and made a bolt for the coffee table in the next room.

As people followed her, the noise level rose and Moira knew she had to make another escape. Her mother seemed to have forgotten she was there and was deep in conversation with the Mayor's wife. Moira went and powdered her nose, taking as long as possible, and on her way back to the furore, peered into the demonstration room. Each of the displays had little cards beside them. Intrigued, she looked in. To her horror, each had a number, and hers had first prize written before it. No. She'd be stuck with the flowers until she was grey and in a wheelchair. Swiftly, she exchanged hers for the one next door and guiltily went back into the crowd. It had given her a boost, something she would treasure for years, but what a lucky escape. In repentance, she tried to be pleasant to her mother, and let her choose one awful looking evening dress, knowing she would hide it in the back of a cupboard and no one would remember it. The other she had more of a say in, and would wear that one.

The two made it home in armed neutrality, and after lunch, Moira tried to escape for a ride. But it wasn't to be. Laurence was on his own in the paddock with scythe and wheelbarrow. She couldn't leave him to do all this on his own. He had cut a lot already and so Moira raked it up and wheeled it away to a compost heap. Amber sulked at her feast being taken away and ate the long grass as long as it stood.

'Your father has said we better get Farmer Grey to come and cut the other paddock for hay. You'll be needing some for the winter. This is such a waste today, but it will mulch down nicely. I'll keep a bit for the rabbits. Shame you didn't bring the cart with the mare, it would have speeded things up nicely,' Laurence grinned at Moira.

A whole new world was opening up for Moira, as throughout the afternoon, Laurence told her all about the farm where he grew up in Wiltshire. Together, they wondered whether there was enough land for some cattle and sheep, his first love, rather than gardening. Moira determined to talk to Father about all this. Possibly his enterprising mind might like the idea of a smallholding. And the governess cart. Surely Tommy wouldn't need it anymore?

The next day, Moira wasn't going to be thwarted, and sneaked out of the kitchen before even the Gills were up and about. It was a glorious morning, with that yellow light of summer. There was a scent of roses and drying grass in the garden. It hadn't rained for a while, so there was dust in the air too.

Moira and Amber didn't care. They were off on an adventure. Moira had put off meeting the racing string. She wanted to explore the Hampshire Downs all around her. They found an old drove road that Laurence had told her about and swung up between the tall hedges, filled with ripening blackberries. On either side lay fields of wheat and barley nearing harvest. An early morning breeze sent ripples across the ripening ears like waves on the sea. The invitation was there, so Amber leapt straight into canter, which quickly became a flat out gallop, and they tore along the lane. Moira laughed with joy. This was life, not sitting around and stuffing flowers into pots. Amber wasn't gallop fit, and they soon slowed down, ending in a puffy walk as they reached the top of a small hill. In the sun's warmth, a lark began singing its heart out above them. The two stopped and looked over the villages, and Moira caught sight of movement near the manor, which stood out as the biggest building near the railway line. It was a string of horses leaving the yard. Possibly she could join them? No, still in the spirit of Mr Hoopdriver, this morning was hers.

It became a very long morning, as Moira's innate sense of direction failed her and she had to ask for directions back when she found she was on the other side of Springvale. Once home, she found both parents out, and that lunch would be in the kitchen. Mrs Gill didn't remark on her jodhs, and placed a plate of salad, new potatoes, and eggs in front of her.

'All from the garden, can't be bad, can it?' she grinned and sat down with her. They had nearly finished when Gill came in with something in his arms. Nimbus was hovering behind him, a puzzled expression on his face.

'I've checked with your father, and it's fine by him. She's for you. You'll either have to train them to follow that horse, or you'll have to go on lots of dog walks.'

He leant down and let out of his arms a small, black dog, barely out of puppyhood, but of no definite breed and no definite shape as she wriggled in ecstasy at meeting her new friends, especially Nimbus. He was thrilled and made a bow, wiggling his spaniel stump like a windmill. The two began jumping about, racing around the kitchen. Moira sank to her knees and called the dogs and soon she was enveloped in a tornado of dog hair, licking tongues and paws.

'Thank you, Gill,' came a muffled voice. Moira stood up, holding back some tears. 'I'm going to call her Puck, not only because of Shakespeare, but for my brother, he would have loved a dog too. Come on dogs, let's see Amber and Laurence.'

Over the next few days, it became clear that the dogs were going to be lifelong buddies, as they slept and ate together, becoming inseparable. Mother sniffed when she saw the new dog, but only threatened consequences when there were guests.

Moira was thwarted again the next day, when she was reminded of the tennis party in the afternoon, and she must help put the nets up and mark the court. Her mother had invited several families to send their children (as she termed it), so it was with some trepidation that Moira, kitted out in her old school tennis outfit, sat on the swing seat in the garden swinging her racket about early that afternoon. Her mother was greeting the families as they arrived, and Gill had been briefed to bring out lemonade when they were all there.

The first guests were a tall pair, Jenny and Simon, kitted out in what looked like new whites, from next door to their old home, Holmecote.

'This is so jolly. I can't believe that after all that grimness of the war, we're having a tea party. We've been longing for some sport for simply ages,' Jenny grinned, and what could Moira do but smile back and hide her feelings? Did they know nothing about the pain of war? Fortunately, the next lot arrived in a foursome and came from the village. The three girls and a boy were dressed in shorts, shirts and old plimsolls. Moira warmed to them on the spot. After the introductions were over, it seemed they were just waiting for one more, so they put an x on the sheet and drew who was going to play. Jenny and one of the other girls, Audrey, were chosen to go first, so the others sank onto various chairs and helped themselves to the lemonade.

'Gosh, the real thing,' spluttered Archie. 'How did you get the lemons?'

'Father is Croft and Sons in Jewry Street.' Moira watched for that look that said, oh, no, they're trade, but it didn't come. They just toasted her with their glasses. Ice broken, the chat became general to the thwack of tennis balls, and laughter.

They were all of an age, all just left or were about to leave school. Archie was belatedly going up to Oxford, and the girls, Helen and Sybil, were thinking of typing courses or going to work helping with families. Sadly, none of them rode and Moira found it hard going. Then the last player turned up, and to her surprise, it was Monty, looking elegant in his tennis outfit with long trousers. He shook hands with everyone and groaned when he found he was playing Sybil.

'I remember the tennis club in Winchester before the war and you always thrashed everyone, hopefully with old age, your game won't have improved.' Moira was surprised at the sudden pang she felt when Monty grinned at Sybil. She was by far the most elegant of the group, with a tight bob haircut and a suspicion of makeup.

'I say this is rather good lemonade, but shall we dandy it up?' Monty looked around, pulled a hipflask out of his pocket and poured a large tot of gin into the jug. From then, the party took a swing as they all relaxed and chattered away, sharing cigarettes and the lemonade which got more adulterated. Moira was thrashed by Simon and in the end, Archie won the tournament, but it didn't matter. For once, Moira was with her peers, those who had endured the war, but not served, which made a new outlook compared to those battered and saddened. They looked forward to new things, as well as growing up, fresh challenges, a new society, and most of all, some fun. Maybe socialising was going to be enjoyable after all, Moira mused as she rolled up the nets in a slightly wobbly way. Perhaps life wouldn't be so bad after all. And tomorrow, Monty had told her to meet the first string at the crossroads.

It was a dull morning, and each hoofbeat seemed to ring out and echo as Moira rode through the village. She even walked on the verges so she didn't disturb people, then she realised this was silly, as the string would come back later. Amber was bemused at this early start, and then standing on her own in the middle of the village. Then her ears pricked and her body stiffened. She raised her head and let out a loud whinny.

A line of ten horses came into sight, imperious, beautiful thoroughbreds, fresh and ready for their morning exercise. They used Amber's excitement as an excuse to bounce about. This caused a certain amount of cussing from the lads, but the horses calmed by the time they reached Moira. Of course, Amber had done this before, so she stood and let them go past, some of the lads grinning and giving Moira a nod. Monty was at the back of the string on an old grey hunter, and Amber swung to join him without Moira telling her.

'I used to ride her out and had the mickey taken ruthlessly by that lot. My legs would dangle like a cricket. This is Tommy's horse. Now he can get his hands on petrol, he's driving up. Lazy old, so and so.'

The two grinned.

'What are we doing this morning?' Moira asked.

'This lot are the sprinters and flat racers, then the young uns will come up. The chasers and the hurdlers are only just up from grass and doing slow work. When we get to the top, they'll circle while Tommy and I chat to Taffy, the head lad, and then we'll give them their work. It will probably be a bit of a pipe opener, to get them breathing well and the tickle out of their toes. When they come back, we'll set some to run with each other over between five and seven furlongs, and at different speeds. A couple are racing next weekend, so they are the ones we'll be watching the most.'

This was all new to Moira, so she drank it all in. Amber, after all her excitement, now strutted busily along to keep up with the hunter. Through the village, they turned up what Monty termed a drove road, one of the tracks that Moira had ridden on. An order came from the front and the horses went into a steady trot up the hill, but not without some playing about. Soon they were up on the Downs. In the distance lay the Worthy Down airfield, now running down as the war was over.

'Did the planes ever scare the horses?' Moira sat looking at the view.

'No, there wasn't much activity during the day. They flew mostly at night. The Navy isn't an early riser, anyway. Typical horses, though, you'd think this lot would jump about, wouldn't you?

No. When a plane went over, they never turned a hair, but if a rabbit or a pheasant crossed their paths, that was a different matter.'

The horses were now circling, and Moira saw a red sports car with a long bonnet parked by the hedge. Tommy unfurled himself out of it and came to join them, as did Taffy, the head lad on one of the horses.

The conversation concerned who had eaten up their food, if they had sweated or whether there were any problems with their legs. All seemed to be fine and Tommy detailed the horses into three groups to have a canter up the gallops. They were riding on what was left of the old Winchester racecourse, but Tommy had the rights to use them, keeping them rolled, mowed and in top condition. There was even a discussion between the three men about watering them with a bowser, as the going was getting hard in the dry weather. Moira listened and watched the horses. It was one thing seeing them in the paddock on the racecourse, but here, they seemed more alive. All shone with grooming and good feed, their muscles rippling. They were lean and race fit. Three of them, clearly knowing what was happening, bounded off along a track into the distance. After five minutes, another three left, then the final four, who were clearly annoyed they were the last to go.

Monty beckoned to Moira, and they rode down the gallop to a further point. Their horses turned and, from the distance, the first lot came down at a steady canter. Moira saw the gallops were marked with small bushes.

Tommy turned to her. 'Now you can see they are all on the bit, but not extended into full gallop. We just watch how they're doing, then I'll confirm their real work.'

It was nevertheless a wondrous blast as the three hurtled past. The lads with their caps turned back and their brightly coloured pullovers adding to the drama. The second group was having trouble, as one was clearly trying to get in front. It was as if the other two were too slow for him.

'Is that a good sign?' Moira asked.

'Yes, but not in the pipe opener. We'll see how he does with two others who are a better match for him. That's Midlothian. He's downright nasty in the stable, but put him in a race, he's a different character.'

And so it proved, with another group, he was challenged more, and worked harder to keep in front. Tommy was timing him, too. 'I don't like putting them into a trial race at home. It ruins their running on the courses sometimes. You should put a few bob on him on Saturday,' Tommy laughed.

After all the horses had worked, they made a more orderly way back home. The next lot of only three were coming up the hill, but this time, they turned to the left. These were the two-year-olds who were being shown their first fences, having been broken in during the summer. The same work, but with lots more bouncing and cavorting around as they flew over two of the brush hurdles that ran for about half a mile along a hedge. This, Moira found even more exciting and wondered whether one day she could ever ride out like that. It seemed such an exciting, challenging, and possibly dangerous world that appealed to her tomboy nature. Monty and Moira followed the second string back down into the village, Moira plying him with questions about racing.

'Hold on, I can't keep up with you,' he laughed. 'You'll have to come and spend some time in the stables, and come with us to some meetings.'

'May I really?'

'I don't see why not, but you must check with your folks.'

They were riding into the yard, Moira having followed without thinking. All around there were lads untacking, carrying haynets, water buckets and grooming kits, in a scurry to be ready for lunchtime feeds and their time off to eat themselves.

'Pop her into that box over there. There's a water bucket inside and give her a handful of hay so she doesn't start complaining. She's always been a handful. I bet Tommy didn't tell you that when he drove to Winchester with her in the cart, he would pop into several hostelries. She got to know the route and on more than one occasion, if he was too long, he'd find she had already gone to the next pub.' They both snorted with laughter and Monty went to see to his own horse. Moira found the box, and Amber bustled in. Water was easy, but not the hay. When she asked one of the lads, she realised he looked older than her father. There were young lads and even a couple of girls, too. They were of all ages. Moira thought about how this must be a perfect job. Tommy seemed to be ahead of the times where he was already employing girls. The lad pointed to the barn at the back and she grabbed some of the sweet-smelling stuff for Amber, who snatched it from her hands.

As she came out, she was greeted with a barrage of the filthiest language she'd ever heard from Taffy, the head lad. Some of the words had been whispered in the convent, and some, she could only guess the meaning of. But she got the gist and swept up the trail of hay she had left along the yard, to laughter and some more rude comments about making beds from the lads. As she made her way to the main house, she knew her face was red. She looked shyly into some boxes as she walked past. The horses were getting a dressing down grooming to a shining perfection and then a light summer rug put on them. She got a shock when she looked in one box. Inside stood two large piglets who looked hopefully up at her.

Monty stood at the door of the main house, which looked over the yard. He had cups of coffee in his hands and handed her one. 'Take it you got told off by Taffy? You'll have to get used to racing language here. The pigs are top secret, not on the ration. We hide them in plain sight. The horses have got over it. We've got a cow and some hens and guard geese who roam the yard at night. Taffy's language to them can be pretty ripe, too. Come into the office.'

The room was in total disorder. Moira saw a desk covered in letters, and what looked like catalogues, bills, and entry forms for races. The walls were lined with photos of horses and racing calenders. The room was littered with odd pieces of tack and boots. On the floor lay a sleeping collection of Tommy's whippets, lurchers and spaniels, who jumped up and Moira had to greet them all.

'Don't let them get too close to you. Tommy took them out coursing yesterday, and they all rolled in a muck heap on the farm where it took place, while he was having a small shandy. This is the untidy end of the business. Have you ever learnt to type?' He waved at the surrounding mess.

'No, but I could learn.'

Monty pulled some documents from the heap on the desk. 'Have a look at this. This is the pedigree of Mehrali, one of our best flat racers this season.' Moira was intrigued, and they spent an hour looking at pedigrees. A whole complex world of breeding, owners, and entering for races opened before her, although Tommy didn't breed himself. Time flew out of the window, Moira saw lads going to the feed room with skips, which was followed by banging on doors and neighing.

'I better get her home before she expects some,' Moira laughed. Amber was looking over the door with an eager face.

'Now, don't forget, let me know when you can come next, and perhaps we can see if you can cope with one of our quieter ones.' The proof came sooner than that, as Amber took great exception to leaving the yard with no lunch, rearing up and trying to nap back to her box. Moira had never feared a horse and wasn't going to now. Using some of Taffy's words which she understood, she swore at her and kicked her hard in the ribs, pulling her around towards the gate. It worked, and the pair left the yard, Moira red faced again, but hopeful she might get her ride on a racehorse.

Amber sulked all the way home and when turned out, whipped around to barge Moira, who was now under no illusions as to why Tommy might have wanted to part with her. Moira was hot and late for lunch, so she got her apologies in to her parents before they told her off. It seemed they were appeased by this, so when they got to the coffee, she thought she might as well ask.

'Um, when I visited the stables this morning, Tommy and Monty (she thought Tommy might carry more weight), asked if I might do a little bookkeeping for them and maybe ride some of the horses. It would be a jolly useful sort of job for me. It would help me with my learning to type.'

'Absolutely not. It's bad enough that you're late for every meal, smell of horse and don't seem to be interested in any of the important things in life. You're turning into a hoyden,' her mother exploded.

'But I've not been home that long and I need something to do.'

'I took you to that marvellous flower arranging demonstration, and you just turned your nose up at it.' She flew along in full steam, and it was better not to interfere. 'You should be concerned with being a young woman, clothes, fashion, entertaining and looking for a suitable young man. Going to parties and social events with your peers.'

'But Mother, I've only just left school.'

'Mrs Henley-Smythe's daughter is already engaged,' came the sniff.

'Now dear, it's not such a bad idea.' Father to the rescue. ' Moira can come into the office with me and learn about the business, ride the occasional horse, and help with Tommy's books. She's young and has plenty of energy. After all, Tommy has plenty of very wealthy owners, such as Lord Fortescue. Perhaps Moira would be useful to them. She might even get to Ascot for the Royal meeting, it could lead anywhere...'

That got her snobbish mother. 'Well, perhaps, but when we have visitors, she must be here, presentable and sociable. And if that doesn't happen, the horse goes.' With that, she got up and stalked out of the room.

'Thanks so much, Father.' They weren't a

demonstrative family, being of that time, so there wasn't a hug, just the stiff upper lip. He grinned with that twinkle in his eye. 'Anything for you, my dear. But I really would like you to learn a bit about the business. Things are going to change and grow rapidly now the war's over, and I've got many irons in the fire.'

And so things worked out. Moira made easy work of the mess in Tommy's office, it just needed time to sort it all out into neat piles, and point him to signing cheques for things like the feed bills and farrier, and then to collate the bills, leaving Tommy to cajole owners into paying for their horses' fees. She got the hang of entering the horses for races, too. It was totally fascinating. Time never palled when she did things with horses.

It was the same with her father; he was a kind teacher, and she began to grasp the enormity of running several shops. Not only was there double entry bookkeeping but also ordering goods, fighting with officialdom over rationing and coupons. Doing wages and getting orders delivered. Two very different worlds, but she loved the sense of purpose it gave her.

Best of all was the horses. A couple of weeks after she started, Moira was put up on one of the older racehorses who they used for the lads when they first came to the yard to get them to ride in a whole new way, if they had at all. Grenadier was an enormous bay, standing nearly 17 hands, with a long back, upright head but a gentle, wise eye. He had seen it all and nothing phased him, except maybe for motorbikes, which he took huge exception to.

Moira found him easy to tack up, but the light racing saddle was flimsy and difficult to get straight. She was no taller than most of the lads. How on earth did they manage?

Taffy came over to her as she stood among the circling horses, waiting to get mounted.

'Girth's too loose. You do it up as soon as you're up. Now get the reins.'

Before she could think, Moira found herself chucked up onto Grenadier's back, and it felt like perching on a wall he was so narrow. She did her girth up and put her feet in the stirrups, which sent her knees up to what felt like near her chin.

'Now, we won't have them too short for your first time. Jam your foot in. If he were to shy suddenly, your foot would come out. Now take your place at the back.'

Grenadier's movement was like riding in slow motion after the quick stride of Amber, but exhilarating, too. The lad in front of her turned round. 'You'll be fine, but keep a good distance from me. This idiot is totally unpredictable.'

They rode through the village, with cavorting and shying, which calmed as they went into the steady trot going up the hill. Tommy waited at the top, Monty being away at a race meeting with some of their horses.

‘Moira, get your hands down, reins short, and keep a good hold on him. You push him with your heels but hold him by the mouth. You’re going off first, on the pipe opener. I want the old boy to keep the other two calm, as he’s not so inclined to take off these days.’

Moira wasn’t worried. This was all so marvellous, she had dreamt of this for ages. Grenadier’s long stride in trot had been wonderful, but she couldn’t imagine what this would be like.

The three of them set off, one horse being the idiot in front, but he was kept under control by the firm hands of his rider. The other was a calmer, lean black.

‘Now, we’ll set off in an orderly manner,’ laughed his rider. ‘Grenadier will not do one stride faster than necessary, the lazy old bugger, so just concentrate on going in a straight line and being steady, all right?’ Moira nodded.

They turned, and without any signal, Grenadier took off. It seemed so fast, he must be galloping. She kept her hands firm and stood in the stirrups as she’d been practising on an annoyed Amber. It was almost in slow motion, but incredibly fast.

All seemed fine though, as the other two were following the older, larger horse, with every appearance of enjoyment, when Moira glimpsed backwards. The pounding of hooves, the air rushing past her, Grenadier’s mane almost standing up, his huffing and snuffling as he enjoyed his pipe opener, created a oneness with the wind that filled her with joy.

'Sit down and slow him down,' came a voice from behind.

So ended Moira's first ride on a racehorse, and she was hooked. On the second run, she galloped with two young ones. Grenadier set the pace. She'd been told to go into canter and then release the bit slightly. The acceleration took her breath away, her eyes streamed and she could barely see. The exhilaration ate into her spirit, and she wanted more. To ride a full gallop as fast as possible and run a race. It was too soon that the furlongs were run and she had trouble pulling him up, needing to sit and give a harder pull until that worked. Tommy just nodded and said she could come again, which was a lot for him. The next day Moira ached with every muscle in her body, but it was a trophy to be proud of.

After a few weeks she was put on tougher horses and had more than one tumble, the mickey taking afterwards being almost worse than the fall. How she wished to work full time as a lad, but her mother had that look on her face every time she brought the stables into conversation.

It was her first race meeting, where she had horses and jockeys she knew, that finished her. The spirit of racing truly entered her blood.

The meeting was at Newbury, and the two horses had gone up on the train with Taffy and the lads who 'did' them. Monty stayed behind and

Moira found herself driving Tommy in his Acedes sports car. Fortunately, she was an expert at double declutching, but that he had the accelerator loosened so not to go over 30mph was really annoying and made the journey so long.

Moira soon found out why. They were driving past some fields when he motioned her to stop and keep quiet. Carefully, from the boot of the car, Tommy pulled out a light rifle; he pointed it through the window, across Moira, who he'd told to wind the window carefully down.

The zap made her jump, but Tommy grinned like mad. 'Go to the field with the picnic basket from the back. Walk like you're looking for a place to picnic. Put it down next to the pheasant. Check around, and if no one is in sight, pop it in and walk back like you don't want to have a picnic anymore.'

Did she have any choice? Tommy roared with laughter as they drove away with the trophy in the boot. 'That was perfect. You'll have to drive me more often.' Moira had to join in, at least she hadn't been asked to shoot it. She couldn't aim a gun or hit anything. Her father had given up trying to get her to even hit the target in the grounds of Morton House.

Before long, they reached Newbury. There wasn't the traffic about like before the war on a race day, or so Tommy said, but a few cars were around and people going in on foot. Once parked, they took tack and jockey's gear and walked to the stables, and asked the steward where the horses were. Taffy and the lads were waiting for them.

'How were they last night?' Tommy demanded.

'Travelled well, ate up too. When the boxes were unlocked, both stood calm and clean,' piped up one lad.

'That's a relief. I wondered whether Mehrali would settle. Right, I'll sort things out.'

Moira followed Tommy into this new world. He found the jockey, and handed over the gear, but Moira wasn't allowed in the Weighing room, while he and the tack were weighed in. She glimpsed the male world, where owners and jockeys talked and joked, and jackets were changed through a haze of smoke. Moira followed Tommy as he declared the runner, then to where Mehrali waited to be tacked up in the saddling box near the paddock. She looked nervous and stamped her feet, picking up on the excitement. Taffy wasn't having any nonsense, and put a firm hand on the horse's neck and kept her head down, so she stopped looking around and getting herself excited.

Soon the horses were led to the paddock by the lads with numbers on their arms, and began the parade. People thronged around, so it was a relief to be in the middle and meet the owners. They were an older couple who had kept racehorses before the war, but had closed their yard, just keeping a couple of horses on with trainers. They were calm, and talked about how good the going was, and the odds. Mehrali was the second favourite. Tommy was busy giving instructions to the jockey.

Before long, the bell rang, and the horses were called in, mounted, and led to the course by their lad. Once released, they cantered down to the start. Moira and the others made their way to the stadium and the viewing balcony, but not before Tommy told her to place a couple of bets to win for him. So Moira did too. Clutching the slips, she just made it to the balcony before the start.

She had her father's binoculars, and, being small, got to the front. Over the sea of people at the rails, all seemingly dressed in dull brown and grey coats, through them she saw the horses and her heart quickened. The runners were now lined up at the start where the tapes were down. They had numbers on their saddle cloths, which had their running position. It was a five furlong race for two-year-old fillies, and Mehrali's third outing.

The horses were sort of in a line, and the tapes flipped up, horses and jockeys leaping away, riders sometimes not as quick as their horses. They were bunched at first, then some fell back, and then there were two in the lead. The jockeys hunched over the horses as if wanting to become one with them. Mehrali stood out as the only chestnut, and she was in third place. They turned away slightly, then came in on the home run. The jockeys began using their whips, some more frantically than the others.

Mehrali took off, even though she was on the

rails. She came through, and as the shouting and cheering increased, it seemed to Moira that the thunder of hooves got louder. The winning post got nearer, and Mehrali streamed into the lead, taking the race by a length.

Everyone in the group, having been yelling her name, now just cheered. They made their way down to the winner's enclosure and were soon stroking the sweating filly. The jockey had gone off to be weighed out, and when the bell rang, the horses would be taken back to the stables.

The owners were presented with a small trophy, and Moira collected the winnings. There was a break until the next race, and so they all went to the restaurant and ate. Moira finally had her first full glass of champagne, but got a warning look from Tommy as she had to drive. She was an accepted member of this group. No one saw her as a child, it was exhilarating. But most of all, what remained in her memories on that day was the sheer energy, noise, and beauty of the horses. Tommy smiled at her enthusiasm and told her that Mehrali would be cooled, given a mash, and once the other horse was sorted, they would be on the evening train.

Soon the attention was on the second race and Moira followed it all through again, but not the betting, as this was the colt's first race and he wasn't expected to win. But he came home second, so Tommy was annoyed he hadn't put an each-way bet on.

The whole day was an excitement, not only after the dullness and grind of the war but also in growing up, and seeing a world beyond what she had expected or imagined. It was late when they got back, and Moira saw how it could be a luxury not to have to do stables in the morning.

The summer passed by, and life changed as the country began the slow process of healing from the European war and later that in Japan. For Moira, it was a time of a growing passion and her love for horses crystallised in all forms of racing. Every moment possible was spent at the stables, but her mother orchestrated many social events. Despite herself, Moira found some of them enjoyable, as she was accepted by her peers. She went to many tennis parties, swimming parties and just parties. Even her parents' friends became fun.

SEPTEMBER 1945

Air Ministry
73 -77 Oxford Street,
17th September 1945

Madam,

I am directed to refer to your letter of the 25th August, 1945, and to explain that as your son's death occurred in enemy territory it is not possible to obtain a Registrars Certificate of death, and it is therefore necessary to presume his death for official purposes, in order that effects may be released, and settlement of his service estate effected. It has been confirmed that the burial place of your son is at Putzig, near Gdynia, Poland.

I am to forward a certificate of death in respect of your son, Flying Officer P.F. Croft, which is normally accepted as proof of death by the Principal Probate Registry, and will it is hoped meet your requirements.

I am, Madam
Your Obedient Servant,
M Gable

Mrs M Croft,
Athlone,
Barnes Close
Winchester

P.87754/&/44/P.4.B.7

CERTIFICATE OF DEATH

CERTIFIED that according to the records of this department 154538 Flying Officer Peter Frederick CROFT, Royal Air Force Volunteer Reserve was reported missing and is presumed for official purposes, to have lost his life on the Eighteenth Day of December, 1944, as the result of air operations.

According to captured German records, this officer is buried in the evangelical churchyard at Putzig, near Gdynia, Poland.

P. Hamsworth
Squadron Leader of Personal Services

Dated at the Air Ministry London,
This 17th day of September, 1945

The news brought another wave of sadness to them all, but with their usual reserve, no one mentioned the letters which Moira's mother took with her to her sitting room. It was as if a shadow hung over them after the fun of summer and settling into the new house; a feeling of things going slightly awry.

Moira helped with getting the steeplechasers fit, which meant much slow work in walk, no galloping. The lads complained this was boring, and would try to get out of the work, but she and Monty enjoyed the time, wandering around the quiet lanes and Downs. The horses were still sleepy and fat from their summer rest. Sometimes, the dogs came too, as they then had the excuse to take off rabbiting or ratting in the farmyards. Moira got to know a lot of the local farmers this way, and not always pleasantly, as they would sometimes threaten to shoot the dogs, supposing they might also take game, or worry stock, but nothing came of it.

One afternoon when Moira was actually at home because her cousins from Wales were visiting, Puck did something extraordinary. The three of them were lolling around on the swing seat on the terrace. Henry was regaling them with tales of life in the priest's seminary. Moira and Jill were roaring with shocked laughter when Puck came rushing up to them all, barking and banging her nose on Moira's knee. Intrigued, they followed the dog towards their neighbour, Stan's Abott's

Worthy house, which backed onto Morton.

The house was deserted, so they followed Puck around the back. She led them to a brick water butt at the side. She barked at the butt, so they peered in. The water level was low, and inside Nimbus scrabbled madly at the sides, trying to get out.

Henry, being the tallest, reached in and pulled him out. His front paws were bleeding, with all the pads gone. Moira took off her cardigan and wrapped him in it and, with Jill's help, carried him back to the house.

'Father, look what Puck has done. She came and called us to rescue Nimbus,' Moira shouted as soon as they got back. So of course, Puck was made much of, with the Gills bringing treats from the kitchen. Father rushed in and got the special bottle of brandy which he kept in the study and gave Nimbus a large tablespoon of it.

'Always the best thing in an emergency,' he smiled.

Moira wrapped Nimbus's feet and drove into Winchester and the vets, Puck sitting importantly on her lap the entire way as Nimbus was slightly sleepy. The vet bound the feet properly and said he would need sulphapyridine for a while. They would have to keep the balance between keeping his feet dry and in the fresh air, and not letting dirt and infection in.

Moira's nan who was staying too, clucked and in her soft Irish accent said wasn't the dog just so special, and then told a long tale about a special dog her father had had. The rescue was the chief topic at dinner, especially about what the dogs had been chasing to get in the butt in the first place. It was concluded it had to be one of Winnie the Pooh's heffalumps as it was nowhere to be found, which caused a roar of laughter, but Moira's mother had little to say, not joining in at all, even though she was normally happier when her mother visited.

That night, both dogs slept with Moira, and she had to carry Nimbus around for a few days. Puck never left him, and it wasn't until after Christmas the two resumed their jaunts. Moira treasured her little dog, who was always at her side, or on her bed at night, with Nimbus too, of course.

Mother was more and more involved in charity work and the church, which meant she often had meetings and would get annoyed if they were interrupted. Father just shrugged and let her get on with things if it kept the peace, telling Moira he just let all her nagging and criticism go in one ear and out the other. He also mentioned that she was having the change, but Moira had no idea what he meant, although she nodded as if she did. He had been annoying his wife too lately, having taken some time off to help in the garden and for this had donned some really old jackets and trousers.

He'd forgotten he was wearing them when

he walked into a committee meeting in the dining room. The next day, he'd put them on again as he trotted down the lane to fetch some bran for the rabbits. Moira heard her mother shrieking at him to come back and change if he was going into the village, but he'd had a turn of deafness. What had been the last straw for her mother was when some photos returned from Boots of an important meeting of the Rotary Club. Father had cut off the heads of all the women. Being so short, he just didn't get the extra angle needed. Mother confiscated the camera, and Moira knew she would get the job now. Father had that twinkle in his eye, despite the shouting.

There were more people coming in the evenings, too. It was a constant round of friends, business contacts and the people Moira's mother was drumming up in an attempt to get her interested in a suitable young man. Which also meant she was often in trouble for being late, or not even found.

The next event was the visit of the Boyle family from Sussex, and on their arrival, her mother suddenly changed personality, becoming a generous, flexible and happy hostess, falling in with all her guests' plans.

Moira had thrown herself an own goal too. A week before they arrived, she had been riding in the second string of the two year olds on their first canter on the gallops over all the hurdles. She had been in third place, on one of the horses less likely to make a fuss and made the mistake of expecting him to follow on. She hadn't put her legs on enough, not realising he had other ideas. Moira hadn't expected him to refuse either, which sent her shooting into the jump. She pulled herself out of the branches to find she was fine, except for her thumb. It hung at an odd angle, broken. She got a fair bit of ribbing too, with comments about riding to a rule of thumb and thumbing a lift to the hospital. Back in the yard, she was all too happy to hand over her horse and gingerly ride home with her hand held in her jacket, more than shamefaced for making such an amateur mistake.

Laurence saw her struggling to untack Amber and came to help. 'What have you gone and done?' he asked.

'Bust my thumb.' And she showed him, despite the pain.

'That's going to mean hospital. Your father's in the study.' Laurence's face had gone an odd colour.

The outcome was a rush to Winchester hospital, an x-ray and surgery. Moira woke up with her thumb in a cast, held in place with a long splint that stuck in the air. No more riding for a while, and it also meant she spent an entire week in the company of Cecil and his sister.

He was dark-haired, very ordinary looking, with his hair slicked back from his prominent forehead. In his last year at Cambridge, reading the Classics, he fancied himself as a writer when he left. His sister was very like him, and between them they could bore an orchestra to sleep. Their only good point was that they both rode and their parents kept a stable at their house on the South Downs. So the week was endurable, but Cecil sat beside her at every meal, when they sat in the sitting room afterwards, when they had afternoon tea on the terrace. Even when they all went shopping in Winchester, visited St Cross or climbed St Catherine's hill, he was there like a limpet. It was a relief when they all played tennis, which fortunately wasn't possible for Moira. Then she made the mistake of saying she had read Sartre to him, which unleashed a huge discussion, mostly on his side. He left Moira behind after the first couple of comments.

It was only at bedtime Moira had any respite; she made sure she had the dogs with her as they made him sneeze. All the time she had the sense of her mother's eyes boring into the back of her head, but she was polite to Moira, which was a new event. Mrs Boyle was also on the watch and when ever Moira caught her, she had this slightly soppy look on her face.

The week was finally over and it came as no surprise to find she had been invited for a week with the Boyles when her thumb was mended. Her mother accepted for her without mentioning it to Moira. She had put on the charm as they walked through the front door and it didn't switch off until they left, where she promptly took herself to her sitting room and not much was seen of her for several days.

Moira's response the next day was to walk down to the stables to see everyone. She was looking forward to telling Monty all about the week and Cecil. Tommy and Monty were hovering in the yard while the horses were being dressed down after exercise. After greetings, Monty told her all.

'We're waiting for a new arrival, Lovely Cottage. He's coming over from Ireland. His owners live inBasingstoke and have bought him with a view to his winning the National next year.'

'What?'

'Indeed. He's won three races, including the Conygham Cup at Punchestown. As he twisted a shoe, he missed winning the Irish National, he came in third. He's by Cottage out of Nun III, so he's got the breeding. He was born on Good Friday, that's a great omen to the Irish. He's hunted and steeplechased, so he's also got the experience. The owner bought him for £2000, with an extra £1000 to be paid to his previous owner, Mrs Kelly, when he wins. And would you believe it? All of this was done over the phone, sight unseen!' Moira felt Monty's excitement, and Tommy was grinning, too.

Finally, a large box pulled into the yard and everyone watched, whether sneakily over stable doors or in plain sight. The ramp came down. From inside came a dark bay of about 16.2 hands high, but nothing had ever looked less like a winner. He was fat and hairy, but looked around with interest, with no sign of wanting to jump about.

'Looks like your work's going to be cut out here, Monty. Did anyone mention he's known to be lazy? He seems to have spent his life stuffing his face. Jerry, come and put him in his box. I think we'll need a session with the clippers this afternoon, Monty,' said Tommy as Cottage swung into his new home with a long graceful stride.

'He looks like a winner already. Now, how was your week?' Monty asked Moira, and after a jazzed up tale of the events, he grinned at her as she complained about the forthcoming week away.

'Never mind, they might have some decent horses. Now, there's been things going on here since your accident. Remember the pigs? Tommy slaughtered them both, and they were hung in the back shed. Two days later, they vanished, along with the gypsies who were camping along the lane. There was nothing Tommy could do about it. He was so angry. They're illegal and off the record. There was a certain amount of oinking in the yard that morning till he told them that meant no chops this winter. Midlothian is getting worse. We're in discussion with his owners, but they don't want him put down as he wins races, but Tommy thinks he's really getting unsafe. Heaven knows what's the matter with him. Jenny was sent to tack him up one morning as Taffy was at a race, daft sending just one person in the box. But that's beside the point. So she goes in, and the blighter gets her jodhs by the seat and literally rips them off her. They must have been well worn. Did she scream! But the worst of it was, she had nothing on underneath. She's still getting teased now, but she's threatened to send the bill for the new ones to the owners. Now, remember Ginger?'

'That flipping cat that bites people, not just rats?' Moira grimaced.

'That's the one. He got Taffy on the hand, so with Tommy's permission, he took him round the back of the sheds and whacked him one with a large spade and chucked him on the muck heap. Next morning, he's back on the yard, but he's a reformed character. There's a rumour he now purrs, although he's keeping well out of Taffy's way.'

They both laughed, Moira wishing that she had been there for all these things, not stuck being polite to Cecil. She made her way to the office and started sorting the post, and noted the entry form for the Grand National at the top of the pile.

The next few weeks were dull, with the only highspots being her time at the stables, in the shop, and watching the transformation of Cottage, no one used his full name except when being formal. Once he was clipped, his excellent lines showed. He had an honest plain head, large deep eyes, with almost a white heart marking his forehead. A high head carriage, but a quite short, well-built neck. A long back, well set shoulders, and long sloping quarters that spoke of power. He had well boned thick legs and short pasterns that could take the pounding on all sorts of going. Taffy said they were like drainpipes, whatever that meant.

Finally, there came good news. Moira's cast and stick came off ten days earlier than expected, and she was free. There was a scar that might never heal on the thumb, a reminder to Moira not to show off. It would need a small bandage for a while. On the way back from the hospital, she had to endure another session with her mother, choosing clothes for her trip away. As usual, it was accompanied by a lecture on the same old themes, so she listened and agreed as usual, having no intention what so ever of doing any of the things her mother was insisting she do. Clothes were clothes. If she had her choice, she would live in trousers and sweaters.

Her first action after lunch was to tack up a now rather plump Amber and go for a ride. It was surprising how difficult it was to do the girth up with a still slightly uncooperative thumb. But none of that mattered as she rode down the lane to the stables. To her delight, Moira met Monty on Cottage and two of the lads on their horses making their way up to the Downs.

'What have you been feeding that mare? She looks in foal.' Monty laughed at her as Amber puffed her way up to them.

'She was on short grass after we cut the hay,

so I think she must have been letting herself into the hay barn during the night. We've got so much for the winter, but she might not need any extra feed at all. She could live on nothing.' Moira said with embarrassment.

As Amber came beside Cottage, the two turned heads and snuffed at each other. From that moment, Amber fell in love. She tucked her head in and began capering about, which didn't help with keeping up with the much larger horse. Amber's tail shot up in the air, and she began to flirt. Moira was totally embarrassed, but there was nothing she could do about it or the ribald comments. When they swung into trot, Amber had to work even harder to match Cottage's stride, but still kept up her strutting. Cottage ignored her.

There was a huge tussle later when Moira had to turn home, but she won in the end, hand aching a bit.

'You better make sure she's padlocked in tonight, heaven knows what she'll get up to otherwise,' Monty laughed. 'By the way, we're all going up the Cart and Horses tonight as it's Taffy's birthday. Join us?'

As if she needed a second bidding, and she didn't tell her parents. When Moira arrived, the public bar was filled with smoke and loud voices. Monty saw her, pulled her to the bar and bought her a gin and tonic. This was the nearest thing to a date Moira had ever been on, and this, not just the gin, went to her head. It seemed that there was only Monty and herself in the pub despite the surrounding noise, especially with the uproarious singing of Happy Birthday. Taffy waltzed around, kissing all the stable girls, much to their annoyance, and he even put a slapper on Moira's cheek, to a roar from the lads. The time had flown, and she knew she'd have to get back before the back door was locked, so she got Monty's attention, who was now talking to a local about hunting, and waved goodbye to everyone.

'No, wait, I'll walk you home. It's getting dark.' Monty was suddenly by her side. She didn't argue, and in the clear air of the night, her head spun a bit as she took in the cold.

'Taffy's a bit of a wag when he's on the booze,' laughed Monty.

'I guessed that, 'Moira smiled, rubbing her cheek as if to clean it.

'Did you get Amber back in the paddock, ok?'

'I had to jam her bum in and Laurence got me a padlock. The gate is slightly loose.'

They smiled through the dim light, and Monty took her hand, much to her surprise. Moira said nothing, as she was for once stuck for something to say. Even when they got to the kissing gate, he didn't take it back again.

Monty was quiet too, then burst out with, 'do you think you might like to come out one evening fishing with me on the Itchen?'

'I didn't know you fished. I've never tried it, so yes. Will it be for trout?'

'No, grayling this time of the year. I'm off at the races this week, now the season has kicked off, I've got a lot of rides coming in, but if the weather holds, next Tuesday?'

'That would be wonderful. Do you need any more help with getting the horses fit?'

'It's only Cottage, and we've found he's quite laid back, so the others can stay on faster work. I'll be getting out on him in the afternoons for another couple of weeks yet. So, yes, you and that love sick pony can join me. She needs to trot off some of that fat.'

They were at the back door. They awkwardly said goodnight, and he was gone. Moira wandered up to bed, wondering about Monty. He was four years older than her. Was he interested, or just friendly? She liked his humour, and he made her feel relaxed, like when she was with her father, and they always seemed to have a lot to chat about. She had her ideas about love and sex from forbidden novels like the Tropic of Capricorn that had circulated at school, but really knew nothing about it at all. The next morning she called Fifi, her best friend from school and after hearing all about her upcoming marriage, told her about the horses, dogs and the dreadful Cecil, then finally brought up the subject of Monty.

'Oh, he sounds a lamb,' Fifi gushed, 'and not too old, and a horseman and loves dogs. What more could you want?'

'I don't know, Fif, we get on well together and

chat all the time...'

'Well, that's good too, nothing worse than long boring silences. Harry and I talk about absolutely everything.'

'But how did you know he was the one for you?'

'Crumbs. It's just always been so since primary school. We sort of clicked and we seem to well, fit together. Although they've made us wait a year, I'm just so looking forward to running the farm with him.'

'But how does he make you feel?' Moira persisted.

Fifi paused for a moment. 'Sort of right inside, peaceful.'

'What about passion and all that stuff?' That caused a huge giggle. 'We kiss and cuddle in the car, and sometimes in the dairy on the farm. We're saving all that for the wedding night, but it makes me feel excited and a little scared. Now, Moira, don't be a chump. You must write and tell me more. I know, compare him to that awful Cecil and you'll know.'

'Have you heard of something called the change that women get?' Moira had another question.

'Mummy went on about something like that last year. She kept on getting warm, but it stopped after a while. It has something to do with the monthlies stopping.'

So, Moira knew nothing new, but she

pondered about the two men. The thought of Cecil doing any such thing as cuddling made her feel slightly sick, but Monty brought a sensation she didn't understand. She threw the thought aside. There were some new books to read, and she still had to walk the dogs, who were much more under her control after the paw incident.

Moira's romantic ideas were scuttled by the weather as it turned cold and wet for the next few weeks, and the couple of rides she made with Monty were marred by her lovesick pony, who became more trouble than a fit racehorse when she turned for home. The soaking in the rain made it not seem worth the effort.

OCTOBER 1945

The dreaded week was upon her. As Moira's train trundled through the Surrey countryside towards Leatherhead, she pondered on the talk her mother had tried to give her.

'Now, do be friendly with any boys you meet, but not too friendly. Don't be alone with them in a room. They shouldn't sit too near to you. It's all right to be close if you're all sitting in a car, though. If you go out to eat, he must always pay. Don't chase men. You must wait for them to call you. Any hanky panky and you tell them they must behave themselves, or you'll tell their parents. If you get asked the question, you don't have to rush into saying yes.'

As if she was considering anything with Cecil! Her mother, however, seemed to think all these were sound instructions by the way she looked knowingly at Moira.

Bundling herself out of the station with her bag of clothes, riding kit and boots, at first there was no one in sight. Then she heard the clopping of hooves and Cecil, driving a grey mare in a governess cart swept around the corner. That put him up slightly in her opinion. He swung down with a grin and grabbed her luggage to throw it inside.

'Do you fancy driving?'

'I've never had the chance, although my mare is broken to harness. Yes, please.' Moira smiled.

Cecil seemed more at ease with a horse and on his home territory. As they both sat down, he showed Moira how to hold the reins and whip. Then, with a gentle touch on the mare, Moira drove for the first time, quickly going into a spanking trot with Cecil calling out directions.

Soon they turned up a long, tarmacked drive lined with tall bushes. On a corner, they came to the front of the house, a tall giant of a mansion built of grey brown stone, with an enormous round wing and battlements at the back. Cecil suddenly spoke out. 'Been in the family since the 16th century, every generation has added their own bit.' Moira heard the affection in his voice. 'Now, pop yourself down with your bags and I'll put Mary out in the paddock. Mother is no doubt hovering behind the front door.' She was.

'Moira, how super you're here! Now come and have some tea, we're all in the garden as the sun has decided to shine in your honour.'

She was led through the house, only getting a glimpse of the light, lofty hall and the huge stairs in the centre. One thing Morton lacked was a place to make a big entrance.

Out on a terrace overlooking formal gardens was a tea table laden with what looked like a pre-war tea. Cakes, scones, sandwiches, and, to Moira's hidden giggle, a starched butler to serve the tea. Pamela, Cecil's sister, arrived from nowhere in tennis gear, and Moira was glad that tennis was out for the moment, Pamela had a powerful backhand. Mrs Boyle gushed, Pamela laughed, and Moira tucked into the tea. When Cecil arrived, she made Pamela move, so he sat next to Moira.

'Don't stint with the cream dear, we run some Jersey cows with our Sussex beef herd and we're never short of it. Now, we have dinner at eight, so why don't you young things show Moira around?' Moira bolted the last scone and got up from the seat. Mrs Boyle could be quite authoritative when not being soppy.

Entering the house felt like going back in time, with ancestral pictures and furniture of all ages. Moira was shown her room, which looked down over the gardens, and it even had an adjoining bathroom. It seemed the Boyles enjoyed rushing about, but she had no argument with the speed they got to the stables. They were impressive, built from the same stone as the house, with loosebox doors looking on to the yard. That was the only thing she didn't like about Tommy's yard. All the loose boxes were internal with a short corridor running along. It sometimes meant a tight turn getting a large horse out, although there were many doors.

Horses looked out on the yard, waiting to go out as they were still in during the day and out at night because of the flies. Cecil and

Pamela introduced Moira to Mary the cob, father's two bay hunters, Soloman and Sergeant, Pamela's chestnut hack, Trudy, Cecil's black thoroughbred, Amigo and two horses kept for guests, both roans, Tweedledee and Tweedledum. Then with great aplomb, they got to the last box, where stood another dark bay, Jack, who was going to steeplechase and hunt in the winter. He had not long been broken and was still a bit 'wild'. Cecil rose in Moira's estimation as he clearly was smitten with the horse, even though Jack bumped him on the nose in his excitement at being turned out.

'Is the gate open, Pamela?'

There were no head collars around and, to Moira's surprise, they just opened the doors and let the horses out. They all ambled out and down the track, used to the routine, except Jack, who had to gallop out with a huge buck as he charged past the others, who took very little notice of him.

'That must save time. Do we muck out now?' asked Moira.

'No, James will do that in the morning and let them back in when he's ready. We've worked a great system out that makes the minimum of work,' Pamela grinned. 'Tomorrow we'll all go on a day hack out to Chinthurst Folly. We'll take some lunch with us. It's one of our favourite rides. Which horse would you like to ride?'

'Gosh, my hand is still a little weak, so nothing that pulls.' Moira was missing Amber, and wished she'd thought to bring her.

'Tweedledee, she's a darling,' Pamela answered. 'Now, time has flown. We dress for dinner, so shall I show you your room and you can get sorted?'

'That would be wonderful.' Moira was glad of some breathing space and once in her room had time to sort her things out, and have a soak in the wonderful old bath. It might have been old and very Victorian and tiled in dark green tiles, but the water ran hot and plentiful.

For once, Moira appreciated her mother's insistence on the evening gowns and all that went with them, because when she came down the wonderful staircase, Cecil waited at the foot in full evening dress. He proffered his arm, and they walked into a dining room that made Morton look like a café. The meal was served by a butler and footmen, and Moira was totally out of her depth. Fortunately, she got the cutlery right by surreptitiously watching the others, and learnt how to let someone serve her in the same way. What had they thought of Morton? Here was all like something from a novel. But what a stifling life where all had to be done in the same way, with little idea about change. Could it last like this after the war? Mr Boyle talked politely to her. When the subject got on to racing, she held her own, having picked up so much from Tommy. Cecil, beside her, agreed with everything she said, it was almost subservient. At last, the meal finished, and they all went for coffee. Moira soon made her escape, claiming it had been a long day. She was now worried that her riding kit wouldn't pass muster in the morning.

Breakfast was easy to cope with. The buffet on the sideboard meant she picked what she wanted. It was a relief too when the other two came down in jodhs rather than breeches. Later on, Tweedledee proved to be a gentle mare, easy to tack up and light mouthed. Moira heaved an inward sigh of relief.

Then came a most glorious day, mild for October, yet with that autumnal feeling in the air. The Surrey countryside was like the Hampshire Downs in places, with fields full of golden stubble flanked by hedges, but there was far more woodland and heathland with sandy tracks. The major difference was the hills. Cecil and Pamela rode up and down them with total indifference, not worrying about the saddles slipping. They climbed up to some heathland, which they had already said was their favourite gallop spot. What they hadn't mentioned was that they galloped down it, too. This was completely terrifying. The horses were used to this and had no doubt built up muscles for it. Moira just took hold of the pommel with her better hand and followed. After several gallops, and several hills, she gradually got accustomed to it, even if she still shook inside.

Finally, they got to the folly, which was a gloriously fake tower that had been built not long before the war. Moira found herself weak kneed as she got off and tied Tweedledee to a convenient fence where there were trees to snack on. She slumped to the ground on the picnic blanket, which had been brought in saddle bags. She found the other two grinning at her.

'I think you're the first person to pass the test!' laughed Cecil. 'We usually get shrieks of 'slow down' and 'wait for me'. We even had one of Father's friends get off and walk home. It's just that we have to gallop everywhere when we're out hunting, so it's good practice.' Moira, while pleased, shrank inside. She didn't really want to have their approval. Cecil sat next to her, munching a sandwich. 'We'll go more gently on you now,' he snorted.

Over the week, they all rode together every day and then took trips to the coast and towns. Moira, despite herself, began to like the pair. They had much in common, and away from his parents, Cecil dropped the soppiness that drove her mad. She was relieved to see that Pamela also had only three evening dresses and rotated them; it made her feel among equals. Moira even joined them at Mass on Sunday. They had their own chapel, and the priest came in the evening. She mouthed the words and looked at the ornate trappings in the chapel, and remembered the last time she had been in church. Bring Peter Back.

On Moira's last day, Pamela had a meeting with a friend, so just the two of them rode out, with Cecil on Jack, who hadn't had much exercise. This meant a lot of galloping which Moira at last found exhilarating, especially as she had been given the honour of riding Amigo. Jack was being a typical crackers thoroughbred and careered around the place. He eventually calmed, and they stopped for the now normal picnic.

As they finished, Cecil suddenly went quiet. 'Um, Moira, there is something I'd like to ask you.'

Moira's blood ran cold. She now liked Cecil, and put up with his weak flirting when he was around his parents, but there was no sign of the attraction she felt for Monty. How do you say no and not hurt people?

'Now, as you well know, we have been put together by our mothers wanting us to make a match of it. Take that look off your face. I'm not making the proposal you're worrying about, but I have another. I have no intention of marrying for years. After the war and all that stuff, I just want to get back to studying. I have things I want to do, like travelling with Lionel, my roommate at college when things get back to normal, writing and eventually taking over this place. But the parents want an heir soon and are pressuring me. Look, we get on, but could we sort of give them hints there is something in the air and that way we'll both be off the hook? We won't get any more people foisted on us for at least a couple of years. By then we might have found someone ourselves or we just tell them we've called it off. What do you think?'

Moira thought for a moment. It would mean she wouldn't get the disapproving face from her mother when she mentioned Monty, and he was right, there wouldn't be any more Cecils foisted on her. She would be able to go to the stables and races as she wanted.

'It sounds an idea. Now, how do we work this out?' They spent a hilarious hour or so hatching what they would say, even practising mooning looks and agreeing to send pictures. It would need planning to thwart two Catholic mothers. Together they snorted and giggled, and to end it all, Cecil offered her a ride on Jack.

He was ready to go, and bounced around, so Cecil gave her a leg up. He was like some horses she had ridden for Tommy, and Moira wasn't worried by the bucking. She hadn't lost any nerve after her accident, either. Nearing Leatherhead, they found a vast field of stubble and looked at each other. It was too enticing. Cecil pointed to the furthest corner, and they held the horses back as he counted down.

They took off in an explosion of speed; the wind cracking around their faces. Jack almost calmed in being let run. Halfway across the field, she was in front of Amigo.

Then the tractor came in through the gate in the middle. Jack leapt up onto his hind legs, whipped around, and ran back. Moira had no control, and he burst through the gate, onto the tarmacked road. She was pulling like mad when something gave on the reins. To her horror, he had been put in a rubber bit and had bitten through it. She could do nothing but hold on as they careered towards the high street. It was a narrow road with no footpath and in front of her were two women pushing prams, nattering away, not hearing a thing. Using some racing words and at the top of her voice, Moira yelled, 'Get out of the flipping way!'

The two finally heard, looked around and as Moira reached them, split apart as she hurtled between them. Moira had no time to look back, as Jack wasn't running out of steam. Then she got it. She leant forward like a jockey, reached forward with each hand, grabbing one side of the bit. Finally, it registered for Jack. He slowed as they exited Leatherhead and on the left-hand side; she swerved him into another open field and lugged his head so he had to turn a circle and stop. The two stood, both heaving and covered in sweat. How could she ride him back? There was no sign of Cecil. The reins were still on Jack's neck as he wore a martingale, so she took them off the broken bit and put them on the noseband. Hopefully, Jack was now so exhausted he would be guided like this.

Slowly they made their way back through Leatherhead, as she didn't know any other way back, expecting to be accosted by a policeman and two angry mothers. Thankfully, all she met was a very apologetic Cecil. Together they rode home.

Jack was so tired she probably could have ridden him without any reins. In the morning, he didn't seem any the worse for wear and his rating for the coming race season had increased. Cecil planned to mount the remainder of the bit in the tack room as a trophy.

The ending to her week meant any wedding talk from Mrs Boyle didn't happen as the story was retold and embellished as the details came up from the village. But Moira and Cecil didn't forget, and did a fond kiss on the cheeks as Moira left the house, which they were sure would give them some peace.

For the first time, Moira felt a sense of homecoming as she walked up the drive to Morton House. She stopped on the way to see Amber, who, in the space of a week, seemed to have begun her winter coat. To her joy, she gave a low whicker and came over to say hello. After a hug, Moira made her way to the kitchen.

'Hello my dear, like a cuppa?' Mrs Gill was there with a broad grin on her face. Moira dropped the luggage. 'Dogs? Where are you?'

She heard claws on the floor and in came Nimbus; he came over and she gave him a hug, but he started looking around him.

'Your pal gone off without you? Never mind.' Moira soothed him.

'Moira, I want a word with you.' Her mother used her no-nonsense voice, so she followed.

In the sitting room, she stood by the door,

not knowing what to expect.

'Now, while you were away, that dog of yours came into season. It was hell. We had curs trying to get in every time a door opened. Then at night, all the dogs in the village were hanging about, fighting and barking. It was so inconvenient and annoying. So I made a decision and took her to the vets and had her put down.'

'You did what? You could have put her in a stable or taken her to Tommy.'

'But he has male dogs.' How did Mother know that?

'He wouldn't have found it inconvenient.' Moira spat. 'There are the kennels at Crawley. She could have gone there.'

'That was just too troublesome. Not to mention the trail of blood over the parquet floors. I made my decision,' she repeated in that stony voice.

'You bitch! You hate me and anything I care about. You never wanted me, sending me off to school at six. You continually say how you never wanted a daughter, especially one who turned up inconveniently on your birthday. It's not something you say about Peter. Perfect bloody Peter who could do no wrong. And now you're plotting to marry me off as quickly as possible to get me out of the house again. You hate it when you're not the centre of attention. I saw your face when Puck was a hero. Well, don't worry, I'm going.'

Moira stormed out, banging the door as hard as possible in the hope it would knock some of the wretched knick-knacks on the floor. No doubt Mrs Gill saw her as she swooped up her luggage and Nimbus's lead, but she wasn't going to get caught now. At the front door, she stopped. Where to go? There was only one place.

She tacked up Amber, slung the bags over her, tied them with some string, much to the pony's surprise and with Nimbus on the lead, walked to the stables. It was all quiet in the time off before evening feeds, but Taffy was in the tack room.

'Hello, what brings you with all that gubbins?'

'My mother had Puck put down because she was in season and it was inconvenient.' Moira blurted out without preamble.

'Well, the old (he said an unrepeatable word). You won't have much luck here. Those two are down in Taunton running Cottage and won't be back till tomorrow. But you can go in with the girls in the Bothy. Marion left last week, the early mornings were ruining her beauty sleep. Put that pony of yours in the back paddock out of the way. You can help with evening feeds as we're slightly shorthanded.'

The girls, Jenny and Sue, were duly disgusted when they heard the story. They fussed over Nimbus and left him with a bone when it was time for go on the yard.

Evening stables were hard work, Moira had to

muck out and brush the horses over and be ready in time for feeding. She was given some of the easier ones, but they still needed to be chained to a manger to keep them out of the way while she worked. Moira collected a skip into which Taffy poured oats. Some horses barged, and some waited patiently. Water checked, hay put in mangers (not spilt on the yard) and they were finished for the evening. It was a far cry from the splendour of the Boyle's place. This was homely and far more comfortable. Meals were supplied by Tommy, so they all ate in the messroom. That was an even further cry from the weekend, and she had a feeling that this was the place she preferred. When she unpacked, Jenny and Sue loved the dresses, so she gave them to them in exchange for some shirts, socks, and underwear.

Next morning came as a rude shock when the alarm rang at 5.30 am. She swam out of an exhausted sleep that had taken over as soon as her head hit the pillow, cutting out any introspection. More mucking out, checking the horses over to see if they had eaten up overnight, feeds before breakfast, then riding out. Mounted on a skittish filly, Moira had her work cut out keeping her in line riding up to the gallops, but it was nothing after Jack. So she told them about it, to cries of laughter about the women and a rude comment from Taffy that no rubber bits were used on his yard.

Second string, more skipping out and dressing down. Taffy showed Moira relatively politely how bad her grooming skills were by rubbing his hand over one of the horse's necks and a spray of dust coming out. She soon knew about the proper use of the metal curry comb, and never to brush a mane or tail, just do it with fingers, then a light going over with a body brush.

By lunchtime feed, she was exhausted, but she had to let Nimbus out for a run as dogs, including Tommy's weren't allowed on the yard during working hours. When she returned, the horsebox stood in the yard and Cottage was being unloaded. He looked his usual relaxed self as if he had just been out for a hack and ambled back into his box.

'He won. It wasn't a hard race. We chose it carefully, but I'm telling you, they will have to keep out of his way at Aintree. The jumps won't frighten him or Monty.' Tommy grinned all over his face, 'now what have you done now, Madam?' She followed him up to the house, where she had to tell it all over again.

'Moira, you can stay here and work as a lad, and I'll arrange it, so you have time to do the books, but sooner or later you'll have to face this. Your mother is still your mother, whatever she's done. Where was your father while all this went on?'

'I've no idea...' she sighed, 'I'll have to sort my coupons and things too, but, please, give me a couple of days while I think about all this?'

'But of course. I hear you have that pony with you. I might borrow her for the dogcart, I'm low on petrol.'

'I had a go at driving while away. It's fun,' Moira grinned.

A yell from the yard interrupted the conversation, and they went out to see what was going on. Amber, by some sixth sense, had realised Cottage was home. She had jumped out of the field and stood at his stable door, nuzzling him over it. With due embarrassment, Moira hauled her away and put her in a more secure paddock, where Amber couldn't jump out. It didn't stop her from neighing to him all afternoon until Tommy harnessed her up and drove her out. Moira was giving Nimbus his walk later on, when Monty joined her.

'I hear he's going to win,' she smiled.

'No doubt. When he switches off that sleepy habit, he can really pelt along. He's not iron fit yet either, so Tommy and I will give him a couple more races, just to keep his hoof in, as it were. He's a cracker. How was your week? I hear you caused trouble on Leatherhead High Street.'

'I did, but it was a wonderful week riding wise. The Downs are wonderful, and I learnt how to gallop downhill without shutting my eyes. Cecil was more human, and it turns out he's not wanting to be married off either. We've got a pact to hoodwink the mothers into thinking we are, so we can be left in peace to do what we want.'

Monty had an odd look on his face. 'So you're pretending to be engaged?'

'Good grief, no. Perish the thought. Just silly things like having pictures of each other and writing letters. He's going back to University now. All he wants to do is travel with his friend Lionel and write books.'

Something flashed across Monty's face that looked like a smirk. 'Moira, you're so wonderfully naïve. You'll have to reckon things with your folks, eventually. Shame we missed the fishing, but would you like to go to the flea pit in Winchester one night and see, I know where I'm going, it's not my usual sort of film, but it has dogs and a hawk in it.'

'Love to, Friday?' Moira wondered quite what he meant with naïve, maybe that the plan wouldn't work?

In a few days, Moira got used to the hard physical work and thrived on life with horses at the centre, but she had a sense of impending doom. Neither parent had contacted her, but there would no doubt be a discussion soon.

The reckoning came the following evening when there came a knock at the door. Father stood outside with a brindled grey dog at his side.

'My dear, please come for a walk and don't forget Nimbus.'

They left the yard in silence, then he began talking. 'I've been away at Scout camp on Brownsea Island. When I left, Puck was coming into season, but the Gills said they could cope and if things got bad, take her to Crawley kennels. How your mother got to her decision is beyond me, and we've argued for the first time in donkey's years. I can't ask you to forgive her until you're ready, but she has realised she well and truly crossed the line. Possibly it's something to do with the change of life, or her grieving for Peter. We all handle things in different ways. You two will have to learn to live with each other.'

'But I'm not coming home. She doesn't want me and never has done. I've got a job here.'

'It's not the thing we envisage for you. I'm not talking about marriage and all that, but about your quality of life and the people you mix with. Oh, dear, that sounds like snobbery. You are my daughter, and maybe after the way things have gone…' Here he swallowed, 'You may be the future of Crofts, and I love you and want you home.'

Father had never said anything like this before, and although it was almost begging, she melted. The two of them had always been close.

'All right, but let me stay here a few days longer. I do so love working with the horses. I'll come back after the weekend. It's a busy one with four horses going off to races and Monty riding. They need the extra hands.'

'Very well,' he smiled. 'Now tell me about your week away.' After she told him all, and the arrangement, he had that same look flit across his face that Monty had. It was most odd.

They turned home. 'Is this your new dog, Father?' Moira had to ask. He'd never had one before.

'Good grief, I forgot all about him. This is Raoul. He's a deerhound and is yours. I know we'll never forget Puck, but this dog, I've been told, has the most wonderful temperament, and loves to run.'

Moira took in the delicate head, the lean body like a greyhound, but covered in grey brindle coarse hair. Very unusual, but he turned and licked her hand and she was lost.

'Oh, and he's only five months old. He's a baby. By the time he's grown, he won't even fit on an armchair. He'll be waiting for you on your return.' Father strolled away with the dog.

Moira was at peace with one parent, the only one that mattered. She was going home, and that was a surprising comfort. Tommy, of course, already knew, and was quite cheerful. A new girl was starting on the weekend, so he had enough staff, but he asked Moira to drive him to Aintree in a couple of weeks' time, it would be a meeting where he met a lot of his cronies and no doubt would sleep on the way back. He also told her lots about deerhounds, that they were gazehounds that caught deer. They were loyal, loving, and totally untrainable. They were often crossed with other dogs to make lurchers, and Tommy already had his eye on Raoul for one of his bitches.

Father picked up what was left of her luggage on Sunday, and Moira rode Amber slowly home, neither wanting to leave. It wasn't just the horses and fulfilling work. The film had been wonderful with deerhounds in it, Monty swore he hadn't known. They had enjoyed the film, had a drink after and caught the bus home. It was all very platonic, for which Moira was really grateful as her meeting with her mother loomed over her.

She went straight to the sitting room, where her parents waited for her. She stood once again at the door, worrying about what would happen. Her mother looked unusually pale.

'Moira. I'm glad you're back and we can put things behind us, make bygones be bygones,' she said stiffly.

Moira made a move back towards the door, and Father gave Mother a nudge.

'I apologise for putting your dog down. Now, I can't say better than that.' She then sank to the chair and put a handkerchief to her mouth. It seemed this was all Moira was going to get.

'That's fine Mother, we will have to live with each other and get along. But you will stop your match making and let me lead my life.' That was the best Moira could do. It got a glare but a small nod.

It seemed it was the right version for Father too, as he clapped his hands together. 'That's wonderful. Now let's have a glass of sherry, and I have some things to tell you.'

The drink was poured and sipped in silence. That crystal of hate within Moira was now encased with a layer of unforgiveness. It was hidden under her innate cheerfulness and vivacity, but those close to her often wondered at the hard side she would show when least expected.

'It's been wonderful living here, and having so many friends around. But, as a businessman, I have to keep accounts, and it's far too expensive,' Father said in a cautious voice.

Were they moving again, Moira wondered?

'There are so many bedrooms here gathering dust and grounds that aren't really used. This is a magnificent house. So, I've decided, we're going to turn it into a Country Club. If they want to come round for drinks, they'll have to pay for them. We will turn the second sitting room into a bar. The dining room will have small tables for romantic dinners. We'll have monthly dances with the Smithers band in the ballroom. We'll have a buffet in the main hall too. I envisage we will get some long-term guests and people on holiday. Another tennis court, archery, croquet, all the usual activities people expect in a club will be built. We'll also buy some more horses, Moira.' His voice was full of enthusiasm.

'There is the Naval base at Worthy Down and I expect we might host some wonderful receptions for weddings. There will be so many people just waiting to be our guests, besides the locals and regulars. I've engaged a couple from the village to help out with the work. Gill rather fancies being a barman. I will employ a cook, and an odd-job boy who will also help Laurence in the garden as we'll need more home-grown veg. So no extra work for you, my dear,' he glimpsed at Mother, 'and plenty of nice young things for you to meet, Moira. Now what do you think?'

Moira gave a small cheer. Her mother burst into tears and ran out of the room.

NOVEMBER 1945

24, Station Road,
Chertsey

Dear Mrs Croft,

I am terribly sorry not to have answered your letter before now, but I have been away for three weeks and your letter has only just reached me. But I am afraid that I cannot give you any news much.

You see, after the crash my son had been a prisoner of war in Germany and he escaped his camp. We had know news of him for months until he turned up in Warsaw. He has been told not to disclose were he was all that time by the Airforce, but I really think he had been in Russian hands. He made his way across Poland to Warsaw with the help of some Polish friends he had made. It was great news for us when he turned up again after the crash in Poland and I can sympathise with you in your loss, but my son seems to think that lots more people may turn up.

So sorry not to be able to help you as I realise a mother's feelings at a time like this.

Yours sincerely
M. Sutton

The following few weeks at Morton House were a wonderful chaos. Father had clearly been planning things for a while, as the new staff arrived within a week. First came Hedges, the cook, and William, who was to do everything. Father told her the two men had grown up together in an orphanage and were inseparable. William seemed sleepy and needed to be told exactly what to do. Mrs Gill was quite happy to hand over the cooking, and just help in the kitchen and house, especially when Mr and Mrs Clark came in each day to clean and do odd jobs. There was plenty of work getting the club ready.

The bar was soon built in the second sitting room, with tables and comfortable chairs. There were new, small tables and chairs stored in the dining room too, and it was given a fresh coat of paint to lighten it up. The bedrooms were all aired with boxes of linen and towels arriving that had to be stored. Likewise, a huge dinner service and cutlery arrived in velvet lined boxes. At one end of the ballroom, a stage was built, along with some curtains and stairs up and down in case they wanted to do something theatrical.

Outside, the new tennis court was laid, archery targets set up on one of the lawns, a brand-new croquet lawn mown and marked on the main lawn. Father decided to wait to buy the horses until he found what sort of guests arrived; he didn't want to have them eating their heads off if they weren't used.

Moira was quite pleased with the decision about the horses, as she was as much as ever involved with the racing stables. She rode more than once a week on the gallops and went with Tommy, along with one of the owners, Alfred, to several more meetings. Thankfully, Alfred drove; it would have been a squeeze in the back of Tommy's sports car. Racing was taking off rapidly as men came home from the war and the government saw it as a grand entertainment for the public. She went coursing with Tommy too, but Raoul, who was all leg and puppyhood, was no good at it. He chased the mechanical hare once, then decided it was too boring, and they couldn't trust him yet with the live ones in case he took off after a cow instead.

Moira found a hound so different from her other dogs. He would take off when he saw something he wanted to chase, he had no recall at all. Ratting and rabbits didn't interest him, he had to run. But he was so affectionate that he filled the gap left by Puck, who was never forgotten. Moira had put an enormous picture of her up on one of the staircases to embarrass her mother and not let her forget. Raoul would try to sit on Moira's lap, unaware of just how big he was, and on her bed would lie on his side and try to shove her out by stretching his legs. He would lean on her to be patted, but he never went near her mother.

Amid all this came the anniversary of Peter's death. Mother insisted they all go to Mass, and for once, Moira didn't have the heart to argue with her. It was interesting having Father there, as he muttered, shuffled, and received more than one glare from Mother. Moira just tried not to think of the God who had allowed her brother to be taken away, but in a quiet moment, repeated her demand, 'Bring Him Home.'

Her mother had taken herself out of the transforming process by spending some of her time at one of their houses, Athlone nearer Winchester. She said the noise was giving her headaches. Moira never spoke to her mother more than necessary and kept well out of her way when she was in the house.

Yet Mother happily gave Mrs Gill and Mrs Clark orders, then disappeared. Moira soon got the impression the two just listened and smiled, then got on with what they had already planned. Father had also bought a new gramophone for the main sitting room, and the two ladies would order Moira to put things like the 12th Street Rag on and they would dance as they worked. It was a merry time, and everything was gearing towards the opening party, which would also kick off the monthly dances.

THE PARTY

Five, four, three, two, one, HAPPY NEW YEAR! The crowd in the ballroom in Morton House roared their approval, and from linking arms went into kissing each other on the cheeks, swilling more wine and laughing. Smithers and his band began to play a foxtrot, and the melee calmed as people made their way back to their tables or the bar.

'Well, my dear, isn't this the most wonderful opening for the club?' Father grinned at Moira, who stood beside Tommy and Monty.

'It couldn't be better,' she grinned with a slightly crookedly. The whole evening had been a blur of unfamiliar people, drinks, canapes and dancing to the band with many of the fresh faces.

The time between Christmas and New Year had been exhausting. The day itself had begun with Midnight Mass in the crowded church in Winchester. There was a joy in the crush and for the first time in years, the arrival of Christ rang in with bells peeling out from every church that still had them. There was much hugging and joy as people returned home. Even Father had come to the service, then after a short sleep, together, they ate bacon and eggs, and drank Viennese coffee for breakfast in the kitchen with the staff. No one asked how Father had managed to get it. Mother went off to Mass again, leaving everyone else to get lunch ready. This was going to be a meal with everyone, the new and old staff and family, all at the huge dining room table before it was packed away and the room turned into the club dining room.

It was a hilarious meal, with even Mother getting pink cheeked as they devoured riches, perhaps not quite up to prewar standards, with the homemade crackers still being pulled, but nevertheless a feast. Everyone had pooled coupons too, which had helped enormously.

Then it was time for the presents under the huge, garland decked tree standing in the hall. There was a sense of a team being built in the friendship. The immediate neighbours from nearby all came round for drinks in the evening and devoured small pieces of Christmas cake. Mother started getting maudlin as she did after too much gin, going on about Peter and how she missed him. No one understood what she was going through, she wailed through a hanky held to her face, so Father marched her to bed in an unusual display of tenderness and firmness.

Boxing Day meant a meet of the Hampshire Hunt in Alton on the Butts, and that was a return to the old days. People begged, stole and borrowed horses so they could get out and, on a cold, crisp morning, the sight of the redcoats, beautifully turned out mounts and the hounds had Moira almost tearful and wishing she had thought to bring Amber. Sadly, Amber only jumped happily when she was up to something, and the countryside was full of huge hedges. No, it was better not. Mother was at home nursing a headache, or so she claimed. Moira was relieved she wasn't there, as it meant she could take Raoul and Nimbus without any comments about the dogs or how she should help the staff. She still spent all her time avoiding her mother as much as possible; the growing unforgiveness making the layer of hurt around that cold core of hatred thicken.

People milled about as they drank the stirrup cup, and Moira hung on to Raoul, who had taken a dislike to one of the foxhounds. 'I say,' came a nasal voice from behind her, 'what breed is that dog?'

Moira refrained from pointing out it was a hound, and keeping a straight face said, 'it's a Tibetan Yeti Hound.'

The fool then called her exact words right across the meet to his family on the other side. Moira found herself dragged away by Tommy before she did any worse. They both struggled not to laugh before the twit saw them.

At that moment, the master blew the horn and the hounds and huntsmen set off. Everyone stood and watched in awe. As old as centuries, the sight stirred something in Moira. The horses swept past, all shining and plaited, eager for the chase. The greys, bays, chestnuts and occasional blacks were a pageant of life. All excited, nostrils flaring, ears flickering backwards and forwards. Some pulled hard at the bit, others were more under control, bouncing in sheer excitement. Hairy ones, clipped ones, fat cobs, haughty hunters, shaggy ponies, all jostling together to get going. In that moment, she realised horses were in her blood and she was going to have them in her life, whatever way it turned out, working, riding or caring for them. She even nearly thanked God for making them. No debutanting, no flower arranging, no tennis parties. She would somehow make a career with horses. When people, even such as Tommy, told her there was no future for women in the male based industry, she would work to make her future in it. She now directed her unacknowledged anger into that determination.

In the pub which had cleared after the hunt had gone, Tommy began talking to someone about coursing, so she and Monty sat at a table by the window.

'How did Christmas Day go? How many of the lads turned up?' Moira asked.

'All of them, actually. We rode a quick burst on the gallops and we all pitched in with the stables to get things done as quickly as possible. Cottage is coming along nicely. He has another race next week, just to keep him going. We don't believe in trials at home, it puts them off. What we are doing is building some jumps up to National height and widths, just to stretch him. If you have some time, I could do with some help to haul the branches up to the gallops.'

'If I can escape the madhouse, I'll be there. We've been beavering away for months at the club and there always seems to be more to do. I still have to send the advertisements to the newspapers and Horse and Hound. Mother is no help, she just contradicts anything Father has set in place. Shall I ride over tomorrow afternoon?'

'After two would be wonderful. Harrison has the cart loaded up, and we'll drive Mason up. With the two of us, it shouldn't take long, but bring gloves.'

Moira discovered Mason was an enormous shire, and they plodded their way slowly up the hill with a wide cart loaded higher than at haymaking. Monty let Moira have a go after she reminded him about the cob at Cecil's house. On the gallops, they stopped and, with pitchforks, began throwing the bundles of pine and bare birch branches to the ground. Then they lay them against the frame. They only had enough for two jumps, as the fences stood about five feet high and one already had a ditch dug out before it. They were in a run of higher fences rather than hurdles, and they looked quite scary when they looked at them from the ground.

'I've got a flask of tea. Fancy a drink before we head down?'

'That would be wonderful,' Moira smiled.

Monty fetched a bag from the cart and

they sat in the lee of the biggest fence as the afternoon was cold. Frost would probably come in the evening. Mason had an old blanket over his quarters and chewed on something green he had found in one of the heaps of branches. For a moment, they sat and saw the Hampshire Downs in their winter glory.

'I can see how you get a buzz from steeplechasing, but don't you ever get scared on these huge jumps?' Moira asked.

'I've never ridden the National, and they are the most brutal jumps in the world. I'm told the first is the worst because you all go too fast, but I've got a real partnership with Cottage. He's a wise horse, and he seems to have a sort of innate knowledge of the right thing to do. I know we won't be coming back with an empty box, which has happened to Father in the past. You can't imagine a worse thing, but it's racing and there are always casualties.'

'But for yourself?'

He grinned at her. 'Actually, I don't give it a thought. All I am is in the horse and the race.' He moved over closer and Moira found his arm around her shoulder. 'You and I seem to be on the same wavelength so much. I know you're younger than me, but what does that matter?'

'Monty, you're not proposing, are you?' Moira giggled nervously, totally out of her depth and slightly scared at the whole situation.

Monty laughed, 'No, maybe, perhaps. But just

now, all I want to do is this.'

Moira was kissed for the first time in her life, and her world changed.

'Tell me all about it, Moira.' It was several days later and Fifi had arrived with her new husband for the New Year's Ball. The two of them sat in Moira's room, with both Moira and Fifi's dogs sharing the bed.

'Well, it was just sort of super. I didn't know what to do at first, then didn't want to stop.' Moira blushed.

'Ooh, Moira, he's the one for you,' Fifi grinned widely, her broad, open face full of happiness for her.

'Was it like that with you and Harry?'

'Our first kiss happened so long ago I don't remember, but I know what you mean about wanting to go on.'

'And on your wedding night?' Fifi now blushed.

'I'm not telling you all the details of that, it's private! If you love him like I do my Harry, it will be heaven.'

The two had been in the convent since they were twelve and had shared everything. As their bodies had changed, the mystery of sex came arrived, but like everyone else, there was little information to be found. The nuns certainly did no more than some very basic biology and nothing on humans. There was a certain amount of swapping information with their classmates, especially those who had brothers, but they had little chance of finding out what was right or wrong.

Moira had seen the geldings and started to understand some of the racing humour, but a lot of it was incomprehensible, and she wasn't going to admit it. She just laughed at the innuendo, hoping not to be caught out. Her mother had never told her a thing about her monthlies. Fifi had helped her out with it until Moira could go to the shops and buy sanitary towels. Then all the girls were in an unsaid club, and they all swapped notes on when and how they coped with it all.

'Did your mother say anything to you?' Fifi's mother, as a farmer's wife, had told Fifi more than she was prepared to tell Moira, but she admitted, 'Well, she said that if he is a gentleman, he will wait until you are ready. And that's all I'm telling you. You'll have to wait to find out yourself. But it is fun. Now show me this new dress your mother forced on you. It can't be that bad, can it?'

So Moira was none the wiser. When she pulled the dress out, Fifi burst out laughing. 'That looks like a meringue. You couldn't even dance in that without getting tangled. It's more like a wedding dress. Don't you have another?'

Moira pulled out the best dress she had worn at Cecil's. 'The only problem is that I wore it when I visited them.'

'Does that matter? You're telling Cecil you're not going to help him out any more, aren't you?'

'I'm not sure. I'm certain Mother doesn't approve of Monty. If I go on with the Cecil subterfuge, we're both off the hook,' Moira dithered.

'I can see that now. I know. Tell Cecil about Monty and see if you can work something out. Now we better get changed,' Fifi stated.

Cecil and his family had been invited to the dance. They had all been hunting and arrived late, much to her mother's fury. They were now all in their rooms changing, too.

Fifi, of course, walked down with Harry, leaving Moira to come down to the dance on her own. To her horror, Cecil was waiting in the dining room with some flowers to pin on her dress. There weren't many people around and she could hear Smithers and the band tuning up in the ballroom.

'Hello Cecil, thanks so much for the flowers. We need to talk.' She led him into the sitting room, which was empty. 'I've met someone who I like rather a lot, and I'm not sure how long I can keep this up.'

He turned pale. 'And it's been working so well, what with studying and everything, I've kept well away from any aggravation from the mothers. Pamela has told me those two women have been ringing each other since the autumn, and even more just before Christmas. Mother even brought the big jewellery box with her, and I know she keeps the rings in it. I've been summoned up there in five minutes. You can guess what she's trying to force. Father even gave me the, 'following the family line and building the estate for the future,' talk while we stood at the covert waiting for hounds to break cover today.'

'So she's going to force you to propose to me tonight?' Moira was horrified.

'I suspect so, and I've got a few debts I need paying off. You wouldn't consider accepting and then calling it off once I've got the money?' His voice was almost a whine and something rose inside Moira.

'No, I won't.' She very nearly stamped her foot. 'Let me think… I'm sorry, you're going to have to propose if you won't face up to her and I will turn you down. I can't think of any other way out.'

If anything, he became paler. At that moment, a tall, rather vapid looking man came into the room.

'Lionel, she's going to make me go through with it and she'll turn me down.'

'Probably the best idea, old man. You can play heartbroken for a few months and then we'll be off to Europe on our travels any-way. Your Ma will probably cough up the money in sympathy.' He sat down and swung a long leg over the side of the chair.

'But what about you? How will your old dear react?' Lionel asked Moira.

She pondered for a moment. 'You know, I actually don't care. She's been beastly to me, and this will be a perfect revenge.' She briefly told them about

Puck, and they were horrified.

'So when shall I strike? Must we make it a public thing?' grinned Cecil.

'It's tempting... let's say you do it once the dancing has started, in front of them, as no doubt they will be sitting and cackling together. Now go and do your duty Cecil, I have to find someone,' Moira stated firmly.

She found Monty handing over his overcoat to Laurence, who was on duty taking the coats.

'Help. Something dire is going to happen.' Monty turned with a grin to listen.

When she finished, Monty laughed. 'This sounds like an excuse for some extra mischief. Leave it with me - unless you do want to marry that nancy boy?'

'That what?... Monty, come back. What's a nancy boy?' She followed him into the dining room buffet, but he was deep in conversation with Stan. Moira could do nothing but load a plate and find Fifi.

Wondering when the proposal would come and what Monty was up to almost ruined the evening for Moira. She even weathered the lecture from her mother about the dress with equanimity, although she refused to change it. There were so many people there, with lots of new members, some of whom were staying overnight. The staff from Worthy Down Air station were resplendent in dress uniform. The Mayor seemed to have her mother beside him and his wife all evening.

Tommy had brought two owners who lived in the area, and her mother hadn't realised one was a Lord. Many farmers and people from Winchester were there too. Two hundred tickets had been sold and she would never have thought they would all fit into Morton House, but they did. It was a wonderful evening. A time of elegance, almost as if the war had never taken place.

She danced several times with Monty, and found they fitted well together, but he wouldn't be drawn on the plans. After more prodding from Moira, he finally explained to her what a nancy boy was, and she felt slightly sick. She had heard of men's men, but this, never. Monty made up for it with a second kiss that sent her head spinning, and it wasn't just champagne. She even danced once with Cecil, who now sweated with fear, his friend grinning at them each time they swept past their table.

Now at this moment with her father, in the first few minutes of the new year, she wished so much that she had never agreed with Cecil, but also wondered at Monty had planned, for it all must come soon as some people looked like they were thinking of going home, barely concealing yawns.

There he was. Cecil came over the floor to Moira, clasping a small box in his hands. He plunged into the proposal. As he reached her, he sank to his knees. All those around couldn't help but see, and the attention ran through the crowd.

There was such a look of steely determination on his face that Moira felt almost sorry for him.

'Moira, please, after all our friendship, please would you marry me?' He grinned a rictus smile.

She acted as if she were in a play. 'No, I'm sorry Cecil, I don't love you and I don't think we will be happy with each other.' She smiled what she hoped looked like a sincere smile.

'Then I'm sorry, and we will remain friends.' He rose to his feet and with speed disappeared into the gaping crowd. As it parted, Moira could see her mother and Mrs Boyle looking both annoyed and sad.

She became aware of someone at her side. It was Stan. He got down on his knees. 'Moira, will you marry me?'

'No Stan, you're far too old and I don't love you.' Without a word, he got up and trotted off, only to be followed by Tommy, who she also turned down on the same grounds and in a louder voice. Then came Archie from the tennis parties, followed by several men she'd never met before. Each time they got sadder and sadder, even faking tears. The whole ballroom now watched, laughing at the parodies. Finally came Lord Aberdare, one of Monty's owners, who burst into tears at the refusal, calling Moira a heartless hussy. So what could she do but change her mind and accept, at which point he turned her down and everyone burst into laughter!

Through the crowd, Moira saw Mr and Mrs

Boyle laughing away with the others, with her mother trying to look like she was, too. Cecil would be fine. Now, where was Monty to rib him for his prank? The band began playing again and couples swept back on to the floor. A hand caught her. It was Father. 'You won't get away with that another time. She'll be after you now. Best marry Monty and she'll leave you alone.' He gave her a huge wink and disappeared into the crowd, leaving a bewildered Moira behind. Monty was dancing with Pamela B, and Moira was surprised how she didn't like that at all. Then Fifi and Harry joined her, and she was swept away into the party which, reinvigorated, didn't finish until the small hours when Smithers said they could play no more.

Next morning, Moira woke with a headache that she'd never experienced before, then remembered the amount of champagne that had been imbibed. Nimbus and Raoul tied her to the bed with their weight, so that was a good excuse not to move. Then she noticed some paper under her door, so she shoved the dogs on to the floor.

Dear Moira,

Thanks so much. Ma and Pa were totally taken in and don't even have a glimmer that you helped you engineer the whole thing to help me out. I played very sad as only Noël Coward could. Debts will be paid and Lionel and I are off on our hols in the summer. What we'll do when the folks start on that theme again, we'll find some way round it.

Yours ever,
Cecil

Moira felt an immense weight lifting from her. She rushed to dress and see if the Boyles had already left. As she came down the stairs, there was a hum that reminded her of hotels they had stayed in on holiday. The dining room, now laid for breakfast, was filled with people finding tables and reading menus, with William carrying pots of coffee to the tables.

Fifi and Harry sat at a far table and waved, so she went over.

'Well, wasn't that a thing last night?' Fifi laughed, 'you're going to have such fun with the club, heavens know what you'll all be getting up to next. It makes our farm seem very dull by comparison. And where is that handsome Monty? I guess he was at the back of all that?'

Moira told her the complete tale, and they all laughed. 'Interesting he wasn't one of the proposers, wasn't it? Perhaps he wants to do a real one, and didn't want you turning him down in the spoof,' Fifi giggled again.

That had Moira quiet for a moment. It also made her wonder why he had been so elusive after it as well. At that moment, her mother came in with that look on her face.

'Moira, I need a word.'

Moira followed her mother, pulling a face behind her back as she went. In the private sitting room, they sat down.

'Now, I'm quite aware that was all a spoof to get you two out of being married. I'm just happy that the Boyles took it all in good humour. Don't you go thinking that you are off the hook now. There are many other suitable men in the area, and you will have to settle down at some stage. After all, you will be twenty this year, a wonderful age to be starting married life and beginning a family.'

'But what if I don't want that?'

'How could you want anything else? As women, it's our role in life, to be a wife and mother. You can't spend your life messing around with ponies and all those dubious people at the racetracks,' Mother snapped.

'Mother, you do realise one of those dubious people who were here last night is a lord? We will just have to agree to differ. We've never seen eye to eye, and for the moment, I will do as I want.' Moira knew there was no way out of this impasse, so she ploughed on. 'Mother, I don't want the things you say. I want to help Father in the business, have more to do with professional racing, or even teach riding. There is a life in that.'

'You're wrong. You'll end up a dried out old spinster that no one wants,' she replied tartly.

'You mean, in other words, you don't want to be stuck with me in the house? I will find my way Mother, it won't be your way, and now the war is over the world is changing, and I will be with it, not stuck in your out of date ways.'

Moira left the room as quickly as possible, but bumped into Cecil and his family on their way out. Her mother, hearing voices, came out with her pleasant face on and said her goodbyes. There was much goodbye-ing and 'we'll see each other soon,' with both parties knowing neither had any intention of doing so, as the plan had failed.

Father was in the stables messing around with piles of manure, shovelling them into an empty box when Moira found him. 'We're going to grow the mushrooms in here.' He turned and looked at her. 'And all that cafuffle last night? I'm guessing Monty was behind all that? I knew you were up to something with that Cecil last night.'

'So why didn't you say anything?'

'Not my place,' Father grinned.

'Of course it was, you mouse.'

They laughed together for a moment.

'Your mother is planning. Be careful. Now, I need you tomorrow to sit with me and look at ordering food with Hedges and then getting out collecting things we can't get delivered. There'll be a lot for you to do, and I may need you more in the shop.'

'Aye, aye, Captain. Permission to ride one's pony?'

'Granted, but be in for dinner, formal tonight.'

Moira saluted and rushed off to catch Amber.

JANUARY 1946

January 24th 1946

Dear Mrs Croft

Thank you for your letter of January 21st. May I send my sincere sympathy in the loss of your son.

I shall be only too pleased to make some enquiries as to the possibility of RAF men still being in Russian Camps, and more particularly to enquire about your son. Will you please let me know his full names, number, rank etc and any information you may have and I will see what can be done.

Yours sincerely

Anthony Eden

It was as if, with the opening of the club, they had been catapulted into a completely new life. There were always people in the house, whether working or guests. People had time, a little money and they could go out for lunch once again, then the lunches would often extend into the evening. In the evenings, it was easy to pop out for a few drinks, too. The weekends also saw the sportsmen coming in out of the cold, and more than the occasional poached pheasant helped with the meat rations. The farmers would pop in and more than one sale of sheep and cattle were made in the bar.

As the regulars came in so often, they became friends. The Browns from Preston Candover, a brother and sister, seemed to take to Moira, and they talked about horses all the time. She soon found herself with another spaniel, only to have Peter Wright say it was wasted on her and should be trained to the gun, so he replaced it with a labrador setter mix, Zug. Then followed a large black cat, Bumble, who was a superb mouser, and stood for no nonsense with the dogs. This, of course, meant everyone brought their dogs with them. There was never a fight. They would all go to lie in front of the huge log fire, blissfully blocking all the heat, with Bumble stretched out on top of them all.

Moira did Tommy's books, but had less and less opportunity to see Monty, as he was away a lot with the National Hunt season getting into full swing. She only once saw Cottage being schooled over the new jumps. He was set with another steeplechaser and the two seemed to knock sparks off each other over the fences. She was sure the jumps looked bigger than before, but the two flew over them with no apparent effort.

Cottage was also being slowly worked as well to keep him fit and eager. He was to run in another race at Wincanton and Moira drove Tommy after he had been let down over a lift. It was a gloomy day and cold, but the going good. Cottage had fairly good odds, so Moira risked some of her monthly allowance. Another National hopeful was in the race, so there was a genuine excitement about it.

She watched with her heart in her mouth as they ploughed through the jumps and several horses fell. It seemed that Cottage was never going to pull to the front; he looked half asleep. Then he woke up, and almost without effort, won by two lengths.

Tommy wasn't too pleased. 'That's going to mess up his odds for the National. I'll keep him at home now, and anyway, we don't want to risk any injuries.' His grumpiness extended to Monty, and they drove home without the usual drinks and banter.

Monty seemed odd, too. Since the kiss and the fun at the ball, he had never sought her out like before and never made any suggestions that they meet. It was most strange, but Moira was too busy to worry about things. As things were slowly returning to normal, she was getting more involved with the business and that meant trips to all the branches, which could eat up an entire day.

The monthly dance loomed and Smithers threatened not to turn up after the New Year's antics. Father wasn't worried and sent Moira out to collect food for the buffet.

The evening started out well, until the team from the Naval station turned up, clearly looking for some fun. It all began with a food fight with the bread rolls and ended up with the station adjutant dancing with one of the large lampshades from the hall on his head. They were letting off steam with relief that the war was over with laughter and fun. Smithers this time had some cause to complain when he had a pint of beer tipped down his saxophone.

The dogs made their way into the fray, catching food that fell from the table, the cat sitting under it, eating whatever he could, then getting on top to help himself. Once they'd eaten all the leftovers from the buffet, the animals stayed and lay on the floor, dancers stepping over them.

After everyone had gone, Moira got told off by her father for the first time that she could ever remember, and from him, she took it on the nose, promising that the dogs would be locked up next time. He wasn't cross for long.

The next day, the first of the full-time guests arrived, a retired major called Pearson, who had served in India. He brought a small brown dog with him called Ruby, and as it was winter, she had to wear one or two coats according to the weather. He settled in and her mother was often found with him in the sitting room, which caused a certain amount of merriment in the kitchen, but not when Father was around. She had made such a fuss about the permanent guests, and then she chatted to him with every sign of pleasure. Father had smiled when Moira mentioned it and said, 'if she's happy, let her be and keep out of her way.' The state of armed neutrality between mother and daughter was, as ever, an uneasy truce.

The kitchen was the heart of the house, a shelter from the guests. Mrs Gill would tell tales of their time with the Duke of Beaufort, as she washed up and Hedges cooked. Moira would sit enthralled, especially with the tales of his pack of deerhounds. But very often it would be spoilt, as Major Pearson would arrive with some awful smelling meat he had coaxed from the butcher, and he cook it himself. Hedges would take himself off for a smoke outside the backdoor until he had gone, especially as the Major always left his dishes to be washed up.

FEBRUARY 1946

February 24th 1946
Dear Mrs Croft,

You wrote to Mr Eden recently with regard to your son, and he took the matter up with the Air ministry. In Mr Eden's absence abroad on a Parliamentary delegation, I think I cannot do better than send you a copy of the reply he has received from the Under secretary of state for Air, which I'm sorry to say holds out no hope of your son being a prisoner. As you will see from the last paragraph of the letter, more details may be forthcoming when the Missing Research and Enquiry Services in Poland start to operate, but other than this, I am afraid that there is nothing that Mr Eden can do.

Yours very truly
M. Malty

Personal secretary

18 February 1946

Dear Eden,

Thank you for your letter of 3rd June about Flying Officer P.F. Croft, who was reported missing from a flight to Gdynia on 18th December 1944. I am afraid that Mrs Croft's hopes that her son might have survived as a prisoner of war are unjustified. According to captured German records, five of the seven members of the crew were killed when the aircraft was shot down near Putzig, near Gdynia, Poland. All were reported buried in the Evangelical graveyard at Putzig, four of them on 20th December 1944, and Flying Officer Croft, whose body was recovered later, on 23rd December 1944. Two members of the crew who survived were taken prisoner were interrogated on their return to this country, but they were unable to give any information about the fate of their companions except what they had been told by the Germans.

I think therefore, it would be unkind to allow Mrs Croft to hope any longer. When the Missing Research and Enquiry services start to operate in Poland, it is possible that some further details will be received and Mrs Croft will, of course, be immediately notified.

Yours sincerely
Geoffrey de Freitas

February was a dull month, with rain and cold spells, which made it more than attractive to stay indoors after walking the dogs. Amber didn't enjoy going out in the rain, becoming more bolshy than normal, so Moira kept herself busy with the club and shop. Monty was elusive, Tommy almost brisk. She put it down to the racing season and left them alone; they didn't come to the club at all.

There came one bright spot at the end of the month. Another school friend, Noya, came to stay for a long weekend. She had been part of Moira's betting syndicate at school and really loved horses, if she was a little, well, eccentric. Noya brought her mongrel, Una with her, who got on really well with the other dogs, Nimbus even going on a ratting trip with her.

Noya got Moira and Amber out by borrowing a cob from a farmer down the road; she walked up and banged on his door and charmed him into the loan. Moira was both amused and embarrassed. They took off for some seriously fast rides over the Downs, with clods of earth flying from hooves and shrieks of delight from the girls.

One morning, they met the second string coming down from the gallops. Taffy was leading. 'Not seen you for a while, Miss Moira, been busy?'

Slightly shamefaced, she replied, 'the club has made so much work for us. We're still working things out and getting used to it.'

He took that as true and nodded at Noya. 'And your friend?'

'Meet Noya, we used to go to school together.'

'Shame you're not around so much. We're short of a lad or two on the yard at the moment. Tommy's looking around again for more lads.' He tipped his cap as his horse was restless and rode off.

'I say, I wonder if he takes stable girls? I'm bored silly at home, and the old people are away all the time.'

'He does, actually. But you get treated the same way as the lads. How quickly can you muck out?'

The two rode home, with Moira telling Noya all she knew about the work at the stables. Moira fully suspected that Noya would go and see Tommy, and she did that evening, coming back with the news that she was starting the following week, after she had popped home to get her things. Moira felt jealous. Noya would see more of Monty than she did these days if she got the job, and she was pretty with her blonde hair and large blue eyes. Monty would soon be smitten. It wore away at her, as she imagined them in all sorts of cosy situations in the stables and even in the office.

That same evening, there was a booking for dinner and Moira was helping as the Gills were away for a few days, visiting family. William, who spent more time in the bar than in the garden, served drinks, and Moira helped. Mother was away again at Athlone, where she seemed to spend more and more time.

To Moira's dismay, in walked Clayton who had showed them around Morton House, with a peroxided woman, who hung on his every word. He made no sign of recognising Moira, and she took his order with the minimum of discussion. He was just as well dressed, very dapper, and she heard him boasting of how he personally had made the sale on the house. Moira was very tempted to put a thumb in his soup and serve the gravy cold.

The soup went down without the flavour of thumb being noted. Then she served their roasts. Now the smell of the meat had been wafting through the house most of the afternoon, and she had already booted the dogs into the sitting room, but they had sneaked back into the dining room and were sleeping by the fire. What she hadn't reckoned on was the couple being very lovey with each other and their meals going cold between them. Raoul, who had grown to nearly full size, sniffed the air just as Moira popped in to see how things were going. She was just in time to see Raoul go in for it. In one side swipe he cleared the woman's plate and had his head on Clayton's just as he realised what was happening.

Moira dashed out and dived behind the bar, pulling William down with her. They both tried not to laugh, which, of course, made it worse. Father came in to the shrieks and there was a lot of placating and free meals being offered, but the two left.

'MOIRA!' She had to go to Father and haul the dogs out, wiping the tears from her cheeks. It was such sweet retribution.

'No more dogs in the dining room, or anywhere else public, and I mean it,' Father roared, but she saw his mouth twitching as he stumped off.

The next morning, Moira went down to the yard to do her bookkeeping. Tommy was standing in the office, looking awkward.

'Morning Moira, I suppose Noya has told you she will come to work as a lad? I've also asked her if she can take over your book-keeping duties, I can see that you are much busier these days with the club and so on, and she'll be here and can pop in any time to keep things up to date. But of course, you will still come and ride out sometimes and come to the races with us, especially the National?'

The whole thing seemed odd, but what could Moira do but agree and keep a cheerful face? It wasn't as if she had seen Monty for a while and she was busy. Nevertheless, she could have quite cheerfully killed Noya. That night, many stomach-churning scenarios rushed through her mind, which she had to fight as they seemed so plausible.

When Noya returned full of excitement at her new job, she declared she was staying overnight and moving into the bothy the next morning. She bubbled away. 'Won't it be wonderful? I can pop over when I have some time off and we can catch up and go shopping. Maybe even stay over so that I can recover from the hard work and wash the smell of horse out of my hair? And I can give you all the news from the yard.'

Moira smiled and gave the impression of every happiness for Noya and the new arrangement. Of course, she was busy, but deep inside, she hurt in a way her arguments with Mother had never touched. The only way she could live with it was to bury it inside in that hidden core of ice, anger and now hurt.

Her father, on seeing Noya going up to her room with Una, just smiled and said, 'how nice, I see you have Una with you.' Moira wanted to sink her hands in her head. She was going to ignore him, too.

That weekend, the sportsmen brought several rather muddy spaniels with them, setting Father once again on the tack of banning all dogs from the public parts of the house. All in the bar agreed, but returned the next day with equally muddy dogs. Moira began to see that her father had no authority what-so-ever although he was a brilliant businessman, and everyone loved him.

This was borne out a few days later. The now usual gang from the Air base and the village were on their second or third pints and telling jokes that Moira rather wouldn't hear. A tall, fat man came in and with a broad Scottish accent, insisted that Father come to the bar as he had something to settle with him. He then proceeded to yell at the top of his voice that Father had made a really dirty deal with him on something; he became incomprehensible. He had his fists up and was going to fill Father in. The other men, in a flash, made a circle around Father and in no uncertain terms, told him just to try it. The man backed down and left. Father was the heart of the club, no doubt.

The next Saturday was a dance evening and Moira found herself determined to have a ball and put all her worries behind her. There were many now familiar faces who somehow looked unfamiliar and glamorous in their evening suits and gowns. The Naval base gang brought some fresh people with them, and Moira was so pleased she saw them before meeting them face to face. The Guinea Pig Club members were wounded servicemen who had undergone pioneering plastic surgery. Some had very pink skin, others had missing ears or limbs. But they made up for it in noise. It was strange, one almost expected their voices to change too, but their laughter and jokes were the same as anyone else who came into the club. Moira danced with every one of them and grimly ignored the scars. After a while she didn't notice, and the evening passed in a flash, but possibly that was the wine.

It became the most riotous night yet, with Father going around asking people to calm down a little and not to throw the food. It wasn't helped by Phyllis having a jelly thrust down her large bosom. Then Father made the evening. Someone told him a hilarious joke, and his false teeth shot out, skidding across the dance floor. The dogs and cat who were under the table took chase, followed by the guests. The teeth were finally found in Smithers' saxophone. Father wouldn't wear them again, and walked around for a couple of weeks mumbling until they were repaired.

As people left, there were oohs and aahs. When they opened the front door, it let in a blast of cold air and snowflakes. Snow was coming down heavily and blowing around, too. Several people took one look and booked a room, others drove off in a convoy, honking and skidding down the drive.

MARCH 1946

Warsaw, 11th March 1946

Dear Mr Perkins,

When I had been in Manchester, you handed me a notice with regard to the late Peter Frederick CROFT, who died near Puck, Poland after the action of the RAF.

When I returned home, I sent at once a letter to our office in Gdynia asking them to undertake investigation. Complete information which I have received are as follows;

Peter Frederick Croft/field pst nr. 154538 RAF/ has died of wounds at 24th December 1945 in hospital in Puck, and was buried at the same day on the Protestant's cemetery with his four camerades; Pritchard, Robinson, Skipper and Turrentine, all from RAF

For your information we add; PUCK is lying about 32 km at the Nord West from Gdynia in district GDANSK.

I send you my best regards and remain
Faithfully yours
J. Januszczak

March was a torment for Moira, as despite Noya's promises, there was never more than a phone call from her, and no news of Monty or Cottage's progress in training. She didn't have the courage to pop down to the yard, even though she would have grounds to see Noya.

The snow didn't stay for long, just enough for the guests to have a snowball fight, and Moira to build a snowman. The weather then turned mild. She now followed form and reports in the Racing Post to see how things were shaping up for the National. In the middle of the month, her mother announced that she was going to Wales to visit her mother in Cardiff and would be back for Easter. She'd never done this before, always having said she hated Cardiff in her childhood. Father, as usual, just shrugged, kissed her on the cheek and took her to the station.

The mild weather meant that spring arrived with snowdrops and daffodils. Moira rode out more on Amber, and loved the Hampshire countryside even more as the hedges turned green, and shoots of wheat and barley coloured the once drab fields.

Finally, she could resist it no longer and engineered a ride so that she met one of the strings going to the gallops. Tommy had already passed her in his car with a brief wave, so she met Taffy leading the string down the lane in their gay red and black blankets over their quarters. There was still sometimes an icy wind on the top.

Taffy, polite as ever, in his usual manner swore at her, then grinned. 'Don't know how long your daft friend will last with us. She's constantly falling off, nothing broken yet, but she's been black and blue, even one splendid black eye. She can't muck out as well as you either.' Moira glowed inside. It wasn't often that Taffy dealt out praise.

'How's Cottage doing?'

'You know, I won't be telling. But he's iron fit, as lean as a greyhound. He's taking the bit and going, no longer half asleep. The boss has taken him a couple of times up to Hackwood Park and run him over the course, but don't tell anyone. He's so ready for it and Mr Monty too.'

'You going up to Aintree with him?'

'Naturally, Mr Monty is riding at Newton Abbot the day before, so will join us there. And you?'

'I wouldn't miss it for the world,' Moira grinned and waved goodbye, her heart lifting. She and Amber galloped back along one of the drove roads happier than for ages.

Father was waiting for her as she rode into the stable yard. Something was clearly making him grin.

'You know Stan next door has put his cows out on the fresh grass? Well, they got out into Colonel Edwards' new tennis court and trampled it. Serve the miserable old buffer right, he shouldn't be such a stuffed shirt.' He walked off with a smirk on his face. Moira had never seen him like this. He turned back to her. ‘Oh, and you’ll like this, the new showjumping team is training over at Kings Somborne. It looks like they’ll be in for drinks tonight. That’ll be something for you.’

Bemused, Moira watched him giggling his way into the house. The showjumping team would be interesting. She had been following it since the new competition at White City and the Royal Windsor Horse Show, and some names were familiar to her. She was a little awestruck.

They arrived for dinner, and Moira helped serve. She recognised several of them from pictures in Horse and Hound and wondered if she could train as a showjumper. They were all friendly, but she surprised herself at how shy she felt. The team, however, was celebrating their being selected, and the evening became loud.

Gill called time, and they insisted they wanted to go on and could they buy some bottles? Father had to say no, he absolutely must lock up. Robert Evans, who lived locally, was up to something. Moira saw some whispering going on. They appeared to be getting ready to leave; they got as far as the hall when they suddenly diverted through the baize door. Father took off following them, but it was no good. They rushed down the stairs to the cellar and bolted the door shut in Father’s face. He was banging on the door and shouting at them when there came an equally loud knock at the front door, so he gave up and went to answer. That was a mistake.

Outside the door stood the entire London Scottish rugby team, who picked him up, protesting loudly, and carried him into the bar. Beer flowed as they helped themselves, at which point Father called for Gill, Laurence and William. They came to help and what happened was put down in the club records as a night to remember. The showjumping team, hearing the riot, came out of the cellar and joined in. There were drinking games, dances when they found the gramophone and much horsing around, which only calmed down as Hedges started cooking bacon and eggs at about five am. A lot of them were by then sobering up, and through the course of the morning, there was apologising and helping to clear up. Moira found her heroes had clay feet. Father had the last word, as he called the two captains together and gave them the bar and restaurant bill.

Things weren't at an end then either. The sound of a furore came from the kitchen. Laurence stood in there shouting and threatening to leave. Stan's cattle had got into the walled garden and wrecked it. All the staff turned round and said it was Father's fault for laughing about the tennis court, so he had to calm Laurence down, while at the same time nursing a hangover of his own.

The same day, Father surprised Moira even more. An engaged couple from London, who worked at a new factory in Winchester, had booked two rooms, as they needed to stay for a couple of months. They had been to the club before; he looked at them and said. 'For heaven's sake, take one room. I don't have enough free as it is.' Moira's felt her face must have been a picture as he gestured for her to help them with the bags. Thank heavens Mother hadn't been there.

It was as if her leaving had loosed some spirit of mischief into the house. The next night, there were gunshots in the garden which woke Moira. She called Father. He rang Gill and the three of them crept out in their nightwear, clutching guns, followed by barking dogs. Maybe someone was stealing poultry, but they couldn't find any signs of intruders.

It happened again the next night, and they crept out again. Still no one. Father was perplexed and annoyed, the lack of sleep making even him cranky. Later that morning, he came back in, fuming.

'Laurence and William, go down to the orchard and remove the bird scarers from the trees. If I ever catch whoever hung them there, they will be banned from the club.' Moira didn't dare suggest it was from one of the teams.

That weekend, all the usuals were in the bar and it was a quiet evening, Father now telling the tale of the bird scarers to his own disadvantage. Moira realised how she loved this crazy life, and this eased her pain about Monty and Tommy. Horses were ever at her heart, but maybe the club and the shop would be her future and she'd never work with horses. She didn't see any way out, but at least, for the moment, it was fun.

APRIL 4TH 1946

Moira was helping get lunch ready in the kitchen when William came in, saying there was a phone call for her. When she went to the reception desk to answer, she couldn't quite make out what the voice was saying, he had a hoarse croak. Finally, she understood it was Tommy. In between sniffs and coughs, he said, 'I'm sorry my dear, we said we would take you to the National and now it's late and I'm in a fix. I've got to drive up to Liverpool as Mrs Kelly will arrive on the morning ferry from Dublin tomorrow, and I'm down with a stinking cold. Would you drive, so I can get some shuteye, and, of course, we'll have you with us for the race?'

It seemed to be an olive branch and Moira wasn't going to miss out on the chance to be there for Cottage's National. Tommy was croaking on.

'Monty will come up to Liverpool late tonight, he has that race at Newton Abbot and will stay in a hotel nearby. He'll do an early morning workout on the course and then be there for the race in the afternoon,' he croaked again.

Moira's mind galloped overtime, but not necessarily clearly. Of course, Noya wasn't going, she couldn't drive. What should Moira wear? Some sort of suit and not heels.

'I'm sorry about things. I guess you and Monty can catch up with it all on the track.' Then Tommy hung up on another cough. All that didn't help her. Perhaps he was delirious.

She spent the next hour throwing clothes around her bedroom, looking for an outfit that would make her look as good as a trainer. Thinking of the baggy old suits that Tommy wore, she must do better. In the end, she decided on her tweed suit and some plain shoes, which would cope with any sort of going under foot. A neat hat with a small feather in it and a brooch that was smart. Past experience meant she also packed her best mac and boots.

Father, still reeling from the events of the last few days, didn't object to her going, and gave her a road map from the back of the Bentley. At least Mother wasn't there to be difficult. He even drove her to the yard where she found a pale faced Tommy putting things in the boot of the Acedes.

Noya appeared from nowhere as Moira waited for him to bring a few more things. 'You lucky thing you, if only I could drive. We've all got our wages on Cottage, in fact, I think everyone in the village will have at least a few bob on him. Good luck!'

Moira smiled. They had been friends for a long time, and she waved goodbye as they drove out of the yard. The weather had been warm and dry for a while now, but as they turned northwards, clouds were gathering. Tommy, for perhaps the only time ever, had tightened the accelerator, so they made good time. After a lot of snuffling, he huddled himself into the corner and was soon fast asleep, apart from the occasional honk.

The driving was easy for Moira; she had always enjoyed it, and apart from a few stops to check the map and get petrol, they reached the outskirts of Liverpool as the sun sank and the rain poured down. Tommy raised himself a little and gave her directions to the friends he was staying with.

The lights of the house shone a welcoming beam, and a crowd of people poured out to greet them. Tommy roused himself, but it was clear he wasn't any better. He began sneezing and blowing into a huge handkerchief. The hostess, Mrs Parkinson, took one look at Tommy and frogmarched him upstairs. Moira was left in an awkward pause, so she went to the sitting room, set about introducing herself and soon found herself with a glass in one hand, a cigarette in the other, hearing endless anecdotes about Tommy and his horses. Mrs Parkinson came down later and called her aside.

'Unless there's a miracle, he will not be at the racecourse tomorrow. He has a temperature of 102, and is shaking. I've called the doctor and he'll convince him to stay put. He's arguing like billyoh with me. He'll just have to listen on the radio. He needs you to go up and he'll brief you now about the morning before the doctor gives him any knock-out drops.'

Tommy looked ashen when Moira entered the bedroom, and it was with some difficulty he filled her in. Taffy would have to declare Cottage. He and Cottage's lad, Sam, would deal with saddling up and getting him to the paddock. The Murrays would bring their colours of white with green hoops on the sleeves and they would take them to the weighing room.

Moira was to meet Mrs Kelly. Tommy suggested she stood at the ferry terminal with a piece of cardboard with her name on it. Typical man, he did not know what she looked like, having only met her deceased husband, who had bred Cottage. They would then go to the course to meet the Murrays for lunch. After that, they would be in the paddock together, watch the race from the stadium, and then, with a glint of his usual humour on his face, to the unsaddling enclosure for the winner, then to the trophy presentation. He gave Moira various documents he always had about him, his badge and a slightly wobbly written letter so she could get into all the enclosures. With that, Moira took herself to bed.

FRIDAY APRIL 5TH 1946

The morning dawned brightly; the rain having blown itself out, leaving a freshness in the air. Poor Tommy was no better. Moira let him mumble all the instructions again, and promised to bring the cup if she could for him to see. His confidence in Cottage was total, shown by the envelope of cash he gave Moira for the bookies.

As she drove towards the ferry, the traffic and people were heavier than she had ever seen. Fortunately, she was going in the opposite direction to most of it, and easily found a parking space. The ferry arrived on time, and Moira felt more than a little foolish standing with the piece of paper, looking at women disembarking.

She needn't have worried. Mrs Kelly would have stood out in any crowd. She was medium height, plump, and wearing a hat like a battered trilby, but softer. But the suit! It was in green, black and yellow, a mixture of Tommy's colours, and those of the owners. Fortunately, the pattern wasn't too bright. But the lines! The jacket had them going downwards, with huge pockets going across, then the skirt, with pleats at the front, stripes going down. The outfit was finished off with thick stockings and brogues. If it stayed warm, she would swelter. Moira laughed, hopefully getting it out of her system before they met face to face.

Mrs Kelly quickly saw the sign and broke out into a broad grin. 'And where might Tommy be then, not already at the course? And who are you, my dear?' The soft Irish accent reminded Moira so much of her nan, who was so sweet, she couldn't help but warm to her. Together, they spent an enchanted morning, firstly getting some breakfast, then she had a shopping list for things that she claimed couldn't be bought in Ireland. While they had a refreshing cuppa, Mrs Kelly did something most odd.

'Now, let's read the tea leaves and see how the old boy will do.' She drained her cup thoroughly, then tipped it upside down on the saucer and twirled it four times.

'Now, would you look at that? He's going to win,' she exclaimed.

Moira looked at the collection of tea leaves, and with a squint, they really looked like a horse's head.

'I said on the day he was born from that old grey mare of Hewson that he would win the National. How are we doing for time? Don't want to be late. Shall we make our way to meet the Murrays?' Mrs Kelly got more and more excited.

EARLIER THAT MORNING

Monty wasn't having such a good morning. He had arrived on the last train, and at first the hotel had been shut until, to his relief, he woke the night porter, Cottage had come up on the train, and he wouldn't be able to sleep in the van. At last, he lay on the lumpy bed and tried to sleep. The trouble was, he was still excited and wound up from the second place he'd had at Newton Abbot and also facing the sheer terror of riding the National. It would make him as a jockey, or he might even use it as the start of his training career. It would be nice to have someone to chat to, and his mind turned to Moira. She was such a good sort; they seemed to think alike and love horses. A thorough tomboy who would tackle any horse she was put on. Unlike accident-prone Noya, who would turn up some mornings in full makeup and get it on the tack. He returned to the morning Moira's mother had stopped him on the way back from the gallops.

She didn't even get out of the car, but shouted through the window he was to wind his down.

'Now, young man, I need a word with you. This messing around with my daughter has to stop.'

'I'm not 'messing around' with her,' Monty

snapped in surprise.

‘I saw all the women you kissed on New Year’s Eve.’

‘I kissed many women, a lot of them married and right in front of their husbands. It was New Year and the party spirit,’ Monty retaliated.

‘That just shows how unsuitable you are. You are a bad influence. I will not have my daughter mixing with such behaviour. It’s not on. She’s a respectable girl, still almost a child. She’s meant for something better than you and will marry a nice Catholic young man, and not someone who messes about with horses for a living. You are to stop seeing her.’

‘We are one of the best training yards in the country.’ Monty was really stung. ‘I’m sorry, but I will not stop seeing Moira. There is nothing disrespectable about our relationship.’

‘Then I will speak to your father,’ she countered.

‘He likes Moira too. He is more than happy with us being friends.’

‘Then I will tell her about your affair with a stable girl. We’ve heard all about it.’

‘That wasn’t me. That was Peter, and we dismissed him.’

There came a sniff from the car.

‘Then there is nothing else I can do except report you to the Jockey Club for lending your badge to Moira so she could get in the stables. She even said it wasn’t allowed.’

'You wouldn't. You can't prove that,' Monty shouted.

'I have friends in high places.'

With that threat, she drove away, leaving Monty drumming on his steering wheel. He had too much on his plate for all this, Moira would have to wait until after the National. She was beginning to mean a lot to him, and he wouldn't let anything ruin their fledging relationship. At the same time, he had a lot of races this season, and his trainer's license to get. He would back off until after the race. It seemed he had no choice, hollow threats or not. Later, Tommy agreed it wasn't worth taking risks at such an important time. In hindsight, he regretted that so much, but perhaps after the race when they got back, it would be time to make amends. With that comforting thought, he dozed off.

The alarm rang very early the next morning, but Monty took off with eagerness through the still wet streets. Taffy and Sam waited at the gates to tell him the news. His heart sank. Having Tommy there with instructions in the paddock was something he relied on. Now he would have to ride the race by intuition, although he knew many of the horses and jockeys and how they would run. He needed his father's experience and knowledge, let alone instinct, to give him a plan for the race, Tommy was a mainstay for him.

They soon had Cottage out for his early morning workout. The overnight rain had dampened the going, and it would be good. Ever the calm horse, even Cottage reacted to the special atmosphere, and put in a few good bucks before settling into a pipe opener that showed he really was on top form, all their hard work coming to fruition.

Monty made his way back to the hotel, going against the crowds which were already arriving. He passed several of the bookies, one of whom laughed and muttered Prince Regent at him. There was no doubt who was the favourite that day. He'd already won the Cheltenham Gold cup, the Irish National in 1942, and had been beloved by the housewives through the war, or so the paper said as he read it, once again sprawling on the bed. His head full of horses, Monty turned over for a doze before he returned to the track.

Turning over in bed, Monty saw the clock, and thought, that's super, still a couple of hours till the race. Then he heard it wasn't ticking. He checked his watch. Swearing and in a total panic, Monty threw his things into the bag, and raced out of the room, pulling on clothes as he ran. Outside the hotel, he found a porter and asked for the quickest way to the racecourse, and continued dressing as the man answered.

'Best get on the train. There's extra running today. Five minutes down that way.'

Monty ran, waving his thanks. Everyone seemed to be still heading to the station although the meeting was already underway, so he went with the flow, even pushing in the queue to buy a ticket, saying in a loud voice, 'I'm riding in the National, let me through.' That meant a path cleared for him and he was pushed by the eager crowd on to the first train. At the station, they all poured out onto the platform, and Monty ran ahead of the throng, throwing his ticket at the porter.

At the gate to the racecourse he had his pass ready, and was let in and hurtled into the weighing room, throwing off clothes as fast as he had earlier put them on. His valet waited with the Murray's colours with the striped sleeves, who said, somewhat sarcastically, 'I'm glad to see you. Thought you weren't coming.' Which brought a roar of laughter from all the jockeys and trainers in the room, but Monty had got there by the skin of his teeth.

Moira and the Murrays were cheerfully totally unaware of this drama. They had met up as planned at the hotel and enjoyed a leisurely lunch before making their way to the racecourse. They were all in a state of excitement, which meant the conversation flowed, especially when Mrs Kelly talked about Cottage's time out hunting and point to pointing in Ireland, not to forget the tea leaves. The Murrays had their best outfits on too, and Moira was relieved that at least she looked as good as them. They seemed the sort of people who would fit in at the club and become good friends. It was a shame they lived the other end of the county.

All around them, the course was filled to overflowing with people enjoying this first Grand National after the war. There were even some new outfits in the paddock and colourful hats. Mrs Kelly's outfit didn't stand out so much now. Everyone was out to have the best day.

Moira's group went to the bookies. Prince Regent was the favourite at 3/1 with the top weight. Cottage was an outsider at 25/1. They all placed bets, Moira coming back with a fist full of slips, as so many people had asked her to place them on the course.

There was no trouble getting Moira into the paddock as the word had spread about Tommy being ill. Sam was leading Cottage around. The big horse looked happy but not overexcited, his honest eyes shining. Sam had done a wonderful job with the coat, plaiting and tail. The Murrays already had his money in an envelope for the traditional lads' present, and Mrs Kelly whispered to Moira that she would put a bit more in his and Taffy's if they won.

Cottage wore 11 and Prince Regent 1, and although he was nearly a hand taller, from a distance, it would be difficult to tell the two horses apart as both were dark bays. There was talk that Prince Regent was the hottest favourite since Golden Miller. Moira was so pleased to have Tommy's expensive binoculars; she would have a good view of the entire race.

Before long, the horses were called into the middle and sheets taken off. Monty appeared with all the other jockeys, looking pale and not wanting to talk much. The going was officially good after the long warm spell, and while the overnight rain had dampened the ground, Moira felt there would be dust flying as they ran, the rain hadn't soaked in. Taffy flew Monty up onto Cottage, and they all wished him good luck as Sam led him down to the start. Taffy was going to lead him in afterwards. There came a sort of emptiness as the horses left, but they now had to get up to the stand and try to get a good view.

People were already packed at the rails as the group got to the stand, but with the binoculars, it wasn't such a problem. Moira could just see the horses coming up to the start, and they seemed to line up without too much jostling about. It was a good line.

THE FIRST GRAND NATIONAL AFTER WW2

The tapes shot up and the entire stadium roared, 'They're off'. The loudspeaker started the commentary, but to Moira, it just became a blur in the background.

The first jump came so quickly and this was often a problem as the horses were tearing away from the start, but this time, the field seemed relatively ordered. Only three fell out of the thirty-four starters, and Moira heaved a sigh of relief, she could still see the green and white arms of Monty's jacket. Cottage was settling mid field. The leader was Gyppo, another one of the outsiders.

There seemed to be fallers at each fence and as they mowed through them, Moira winced and hoped the horses weren't hurt, remembering how tough the branches had been when she had helped to build the jumps. It was dusty too. She saw it flying into the air as the field charged over the jumps. Prince Regent was near the front.

Becher's Brook, the huge rail and brook, was the sixth jump and her heart leapt into her mouth. This was one of the most feared obstacles. One horse flew over and cartwheeled. She saw it land on its head and lay still, it must have broken its neck. She felt sick for the horse and sad for the owner going home with an empty van.

Lough Conn had gone into the lead at the left-handed Canal turn and for a while had a lead of four lengths. He was the first over Valentine's Brook. Then it was the Chair before the water jump, and the crowds roared as the field turned towards the stands, then back to the country, and the second time round.

At the 19th fence, there was a gap in the greenery, which many riders aimed for, but they all seemed to fall going through it. Something caught them out as they jumped through. The loose horses were becoming a real menace, even though some filtered off naturally. Moira was torn between looking at all the runners and keeping her eye on Cottage, she had to readjust constantly her tiny view as they sped by.

The Second Becher's had three more fallers, but 1 and 11 were still there. Limestone Edward was now in the lead, after Lough Conn had fallen at the 16th. He kept that until Valentines, where Prince Regent began his race, going into the lead, his jockey looking back to see who was behind.

At the last fence, it was Prince Regent and Jack Finlay. It really seemed that Prince Regent was running out of steam as he seemed to slow, then suddenly from the behind came Cottage.

In the last furlongs, he made the break for it and swept ahead, winning by four lengths with Jack Finlay, a 100/1 outsider coming in second, Prince Regent third. The crowds went mad, bursting into a tremendous roar, whether excitement or disappointment. An amazing race had been run.

Moira was cheering with excitement, and even hugged the Murrays. Everyone was exclaiming what a wonderful horse, what a ride. But not all were so happy, those who had betted on Prince Regent.

The four fought their way down to the winner's enclosure. It was only when they got there that they realised Mrs Kelly had disappeared. Two police horses were escorting a widely grinning Monty in through the crowds, all of whom were trying to pat or congratulate the winner. Cottage was blowing, but didn't look exhausted. As they came into the crowded enclosure, Moira noticed an annoyed Taffy walking beside Cottage, because leading him in was a Mrs Kelly with a broad smile on her face.

To Moira's relief, the Murrays burst out laughing when they saw this and when Cottage reached the enclosure, she gave the reins to Taffy, so he did the last stretch after all.

'I expect she'll still want that thousand pounds I owe her now he's won,' was Mr Murray's dry comment, but he smiled broadly. Monty flew off Cottage, and once Taffy had unsaddled him, he took the saddle to weigh out, giving Cottage a big kiss on the neck, much to the approval of the crowd.

Cottage was then led off, and the crowd moved to the area where the trophy would be presented. They didn't have to wait long, and Moira took photos of everyone with her camera. She managed to keep out of the way of all the reporters too. She wondered if Tommy's temperature had gone up or down as he listened to the race.

It was all a whirlwind, and she found herself exhausted by the time she had said the farewells to the Murrays and driven Mrs Kelly to the ferry, not forgetting all the shopping in the boot. She also collected a lot of money from the bookies, who were more than cheerful that Prince Regent, as a hot favourite had lost and they wouldn't be made homeless with the payout.

Then it was a drive to the Parkinson's house where a still very wheezy Tommy sat drinking a small champagne, insisting he would be well enough to travel home in the morning. Monty had disappeared. There were rumours of a party in the pub the jockeys favoured and he would return sometime. Cottage would be on the first train the next day.

RETURNING HOME

Moira bought every newspaper she could the next morning, and they all pored over the pictures and reports. Then it was time to drive home. Tommy seemed much better; it seemed the excitement had put the illness on its head. He was pleased he had made the headlines, just for not being there.

'Now,' he said in a slightly croaky voice. 'We'll have more horses coming in for training and Monty will have more rides, unless he goes completely over to helping me with the training.' He mused for a moment. 'We might need some more help from you, too. You know Noya is slightly scatterbrained.'

'She always was at school.' They laughed as if that time when they had both withdrawn from her had never happened. When they got to the stables, all the lads cheered. They had timed it well, as Cottage had just arrived, the van being followed by a convoy of cars from Winchester. There were press and people, as ever, wanting to give Cottage a pat or a treat. He took it all with great humour.

Moira found her father at her side. 'How wonderful! Tommy rang me earlier. There's going to be a big party up at the club tomorrow afternoon, any excuse for a knees -up,' he laughed.

Moira heard Tommy announcing it and waved as she got in the Bentley, clutching her mountain of newspapers.

And so it was. At two pm, Cottage was led up through the village and paraded on the further end of the main lawn to much cheering and acclamation. It seemed much of Winchester had come, even the Mayor and the councillors. Moira saw her mother looking very officious standing with them. Monty sat proudly in his Murray's colours and there was talk of a portrait being commissioned. After a couple of hours, it was enough for Cottage, and Monty went to ride him back to the yard.

Moira hadn't spoken to him at all. Their paths hadn't crossed, but she also had a sense he was still avoiding her. So it was a surprise when he caught her eye. 'Moira, take this jacket for me. I'm not wearing it through the village again. We've had enough attention. Why don't you get Amber and ride with me? I want to talk to you.'

Together, they rode back, a few small boys following them until Monty told them there was lots of food back at the club. Amber, not being in season, didn't flirt with Cottage, but the two sniffed each other and walked together in peace. There was a silence to fill.

'Will Cottage be turned away now?' asked Moira.

'I think so, at least until June, when we'll be back to a fat, hairy slug to get fit,' Monty laughed.

'I'll be glad of a break too, but there's already been several calls for me to ride. The season can't finish too quickly for me though, it's been quite a tough one.'

'Tell me about the race.'

'First, let me tell you about before it started.' When he had finished about his unexpected lie-in, he continued. 'The start was good. I knew it would be best to keep mid field at least for the first round. Cottage was full of himself, in fact, he felt like a bomb that might explode, but controllable. The dust was awful where we were at the back. The water jump almost tempted me to land in it. I thought Lough Conn might just do it, even though he went to the front too soon. Those loose horses became a nightmare. One jumped and swerved in front of me. You should have heard the language when they all began falling in that gap. I pushed to the side when I saw the direction they were headed. It's funny, there was an almost calm feeling, just like the pair of us were biding our time, getting around safely and then to go for it. When Limestone Jack took the lead though, I began to worry, I had been making steady progress until then. The two looked like they would battle it out and I wouldn't get a chance to go through. Then at the fifth last, Limestone Jack jumped badly, and that took the stuffing out of him. Prince Regent took the lead. My heart dived into my boots.'

'Between Melling Road and the second last,

I saw Hyde look around, and I knew something was up. I set Cottage alight, and he flew like that released bomb. I was only a length down. I just needed to jump safely to get to Prince Regent. I think I rode about three finishes in those last furlongs. Jack Finlay was catching up, too. He had me worried for a while. I saw Prince Regent was out on his feet, stone cold. Hyde wasn't giving him a breather, and the horse was no longer on his bit. Oh, Moira, it's such a shame you can't ride in a race. That feeling of first past the post is the best in the world.'

Moira was caught up in seeing the race and wishing she were there. 'Maybe things will change as the world will now the war is over,' she replied a little glumly.

'Cheer up, things are going to be better now. There's something I need to tell you. I'm sorry that Tommy and I have been slightly off lately. Let me tell you why…'

Moira had to fight back even more fury when she heard about her mother's interference, but Monty continued, 'but now we don't care, Moira. You are more than a pal, and we will be seeing more of each other. Oh, heck, Cottage, move over.' He leant down and kissed her firmly on the lips, not even slipping on the tiny saddle. They both laughed, and making grand plans for the future, rode into the yard, where Amber was rewarded with a night in the box next to Cottage. Moira and Monty went to the Cart and Horses and talked even more until closing time.

The crowds soon went home when Cottage and Tommy left. He wasn't quite as fit as he thought. After clearing up outside, everyone disappeared, leaving Father and Mother on their own for the first time in many months. It was getting late, and they both yawned.

'Well, that wasn't so bad, was it?' asked Father.

'I would have preferred it not to be on a Sunday, but it's over now.' She replied, still a little annoyed.

'We haven't had a holiday for ages. How about we go down to that comfortable hotel in Torquay? I'm sure they will be open again now,' he said with a smile.

'That might be pleasant. Now, I must tell you about the letter I received just before I went away.'

At that point, Gill came in, 'I'm sorry Sir and Madam, but there's some visitors, a couple with a baby, and they're absolutely sure you'll want to see them. Shall I bring them in?'

'No, we'll come out, come on, Mother, when they've gone, I'll ring that hotel.'

MIDDLE

PUTZIG, POLAND, 1939

The German invasion of the quiet town of Puck, which lies on the coast of the Baltic sea, northwest of Dansk, came as a tremendous shock, despite all the warnings, politics and sabre rattling that had been going on the past few years. It began with bombing on the morning of Friday 21st September. The Naval Airbase and the Airforce units stationed there were wrecked. Puck became German Putzig.

The Nazis marched in with an ideology of hatred carried by heavy weaponry and brutality. By November, they rounded up nearly every resident, interrogated them, then either murdered or deported to concentration camps. The motherland was trying to exterminate an entire population.

The farmers were also detained, leaving crops and livestock to fend for themselves. One dairy farmer, Piotr Nowak, was being 'processed' when a tremendous commotion erupted outside, which halted proceedings.

'It is totally insufferable that this has been so badly managed by the Third Reich that there is no fresh milk or cream for my morning coffee.' Oberst Schmidt, who was in charge of everything, was bellowing at the top of his voice. He made life a misery not only for the Polish but also for his men.

Piotr, who thought quickly in his total fear, and knowing he had nothing to lose, shouted out in bad German, 'I have milk.'

That had all the men in the room turn to him, and the Polish speaker demanded an explanation.

'I have the largest dairy herd, and we have supplied the town for years. If you will let me go, I will milk a cow and bring cream and butter, too.'

They lifted him off the chair and frogmarched him out of the building, into a transport vehicle and to his farm. He snatched his hands free from those holding him and they followed him into the dairy. He pointed to the slabs of prepared butter and jugs of cream. But there was no fresh milk because he had been incarcerated for three days. They tried to stop him, so he shouted 'cows' at them, so they followed him as he went to the yard, and shoved the nearest bursting cow into the stall. The milk gushed, and he soon had an overflowing pail. Again, they leapt forward and tried to grab him as he poured it through a sieve to filter out any bits and pieces.

They all then bundled into the vehicle. Much to Piotr's relief, they missed him opening the gate to let the cows out. They could eat and might survive if he never returned. The whole situation could have been comical if Piotr hadn't been so utterly terrified.

It seemed his interrogation was over, and they threw him back into the prison. He sent a shouted message down the corridor of cells to his wife, telling her all that had happened. The next morning he was hauled out, not into the interrogation room, but into the office of the Oberst.

'You will remain here as a slave, producing milk and dairy products for the Third Reich. Each day, you will bring milk and products to the kitchen. If you miss a day, you will join the others on the trains,' the Oberst barked.

'Sir, if you want products, I need my wife to serve me as she makes the cheese and butter.'

'See to it,' The Oberst snarled at his men.

So, for the next few years of the war, Piotr and Marta, his wife, were allowed to continue on their farm in the hamlet of Połczyno on the edge of the town. Not that life was easy. They had no money and needed to beg and barter for things, but they had the advantage of the milk. They heard of deportations from some of the few townspeople they spoke to when delivering. They also heard sounds of gunfire in the woods. Some sort of camp was built on the edges of the town. They received frequent visits from soldiers, and their food was often taken away. Piotr, on more than one occasion, was imprisoned for no apparent reason, but it usually ended when their milk ran out.

DECEMBER 18TH 1944

RAF Metheringham

Peter knew this raid was going to be a big one, but after so many raids that were, if anything routine, he felt in this one there was an element of safety in numbers. Two hundred and thirty-six Lancasters of the Pathfinder squadrons would fly. The good humoured briefing told them they would attack the port of Gdynia or Gotenhafen, as the Germans named it, to destroy the remainder of the fleet anchored there. They would fly over Denmark, crossing the west coast, hopefully with little opposition, as there would be a lot of cloud that night. It wouldn't be as long a mission as some; the port lay on the Baltic coast, and that was a relief. They would soon be at their target, then it would be a quick drop of the bombs and home.

All too soon, in the evening dusk, the seven crew bundled into the truck and bumped down the airfield to the planes. Once they jumped out, came the worst time of every mission. It didn't help that with the now customary night bombing flights, they always seemed to stand in an icy wind. Everyone hated this wait with every bone of their bodies and arguments broke out. Peter held his rosary in a pocket and said it to himself, trying to keep out of everyone's way, when at last the order came to go. The fear and hate vanished as they climbed aboard and all got into the preparation for takeoff. Peter sorted out his maps, checked the camera and programmed the mechanical bombing computer for the bomb load. Then he squirmed around to get comfortable. His place below the front gunner was in a tiny area which looked forwards through a small perspex blister. Cold air always steamed through from the wind coming in from the gun turret. Oxygen ready to be connected, they took off.

As ever, it seemed the plane would never get there as it rumbled down the runway, then came the heart lurching moment when it leapt into the air and was away.

The flight was uneventful. They crossed the English coast at 19.22 and they were on time. Soon they saw the port because of the rings of searchlights. Peter had everything plotted, mapped, and the bombs just needed arming.

As they drew near the coast, Peter took over the controls of the plane. Around them streamed the red and yellow tracer shells coming from the flak batteries. The searchlights were blinding and all over them. Ahead of him, other planes dropped their loads, and the pressure waves from the explosions made the plane cavort in the air. Things flew around the cabin. Peter kept the crew aware of how he was getting on in his sights, 'left, right, left, down, steady… at last,' he shouted and pressed the button then; 'Bombs are gone!'

Skipper took the aiming point photo then he took over the controls, and they turned northwards to fly back over Denmark. The crew didn't relax; they were still being buffeted by the percussion waves and had to watch out for the rest of their flight around them.

From nowhere, came a burst of fire as a Junker 88 fighter attacked from beneath them. The 20mm cannon shells ripped through the fuselage and into the left wing. Peter's Lancaster flew at the rear of his section, and in seconds, the wing caught alight, making the plane career southwards.

Everyone leapt into well-rehearsed action plans, the engine fire extinguishers were activated and Skipper flicked the damaged engine kill switch. All was to no avail. They headed towards the ground, losing about 4,000 feet in what seemed like seconds. The violent force of the dive pinned them all in pace. No one could move.

'Can we land, Peter?' Skipper shouted.

Peter was ahead of him. 'To the east of Putzig it's all flat farmland, aim for there.'

There came another round of shells and they ripped through the floor of the cockpit, shattering Peter's perspex blister. The wind roared around him, and all he could smell was the reek of cordite. It was chaos, smoke, and flames. He couldn't hear the crew anymore except for incoherent yelling. He released himself and crawled rearwards until he found an open hatch and jumped. It seemed the thing to do. As he flew out, bizarrely, he noticed his watch said 22.12. They should have been well on the way home by now.

Peter pulled his parachute cord as soon as he felt free of the plane. It roared past him with a grinding of breaking metal and as he came down, there was a colossal explosion as the plane hit the ground and flew along the earth in a ball of flame. The back draft threw a shock wave into the air and Peter found himself lifted, and then something solid hit his back and ripped it. He fell to the ground, which was cold, hard, and quiet.

He did not know how long he had been lying there; he heard some shouting, but the pain was so bad, he didn't care. Someone tugged violently at him, pulling off the parachute, flying gear, and now his clothing. Even in his bemused state, he knew something wasn't right with this and resisted. A woman's voice in an unknown language shouted at him, then came a slap and he fell unconscious again.

A light shone in his eyes. Was he in heaven or hospital? Peter tried to sit up, but found he lay on his side and couldn't move. Again, that voice, admonishing he was sure, but what for he couldn't imagine. Then it occurred to him to open his eyes.

There was a woman peering at him, which made him jump. She wore a tattered dress with bodice and an apron and some sort of cloth around her head. She put her fingers to her mouth, that much he could understand.

She pulled a faded picture of a married couple out of the dress and pointed to the woman, making it clear that it was herself. Then the man. She pointed at the sky, followed by an impersonation of a plane swooping to the ground. Then the garotting around her throat and pretending to die, like a child would do in a game. She pointed again at the man and woman in the picture. Peter got it. Her husband had been killed in his air crash. She now pointed at himself, and looking down, Peter realised he wasn't in uniform, but baggy, smelly clothes that reeked of some sort of animal. He felt his neck, the dog tags were gone. She now pointed again at her husband. The enormity of what she had done hit Peter like a thunderbolt, and he was gone again.

The next thing he found out when he came to was that she was rubbing something into his hair and it smelled like beetroot. When she saw his eyes open, the picture came out and this time she pointed at her husband's head. Wrong hair colour. This time, Peter stayed awake. The pain in his back was bad, but he could live with it. She saw him arch his back and made a calming motion. She got some paper and drew a tree, a branch and pointed to his back. He had been injured by a branch of a tree. He must have fallen through it to the ground. That would make a joke in the mess, a branch rescue.

That brought him back. He grabbed the paper himself and drew a stick plane and seven stick men. She got it. Two she pointed to at the back, and she ran with her fingers, then grabbed them. Two survived but had been caught. She pointed at him, then pointed at the four other stick men and made a sad face. Peter sank back, but at least some of them had survived.

She was still there and so he pointed to himself and said, 'Peter.'

She frowned and shook her head. 'Piotr Nowak.'

Then herself, 'Marta Nowak.'

Through the night, they learnt rapidly from each other, Peter having a few Polish words from the airmen he had served with. He found he was on a small dairy farm in a hamlet called Połczyno, near Puck (Marta refused to call it Putzig) on the Baltic coast, and that scared him. They had been given intelligence on the Nazi occupation of the entire region several times. The farm supplied milk to the Germans, but he didn't really understand how they managed it and avoided the grim fate of many. There had been rumours of mass deportations, massacres, and she told him about the concentration camp and POW camp nearby.

He made a despairing sound, and face, but again, she made it clear; he was Piotr, and safe. She showed him the wound on his back by using two small mirrors. A deep cut ran right down his back and it now throbbed. She applied some salve and bound it up again. He got the idea that perhaps she was applying things normally used to heal cows, but he believed they would work. Peter found it difficult when she nursed him, he had never been touched by a woman of his own age. Marta told him several times that she had known there would be only a few minutes to change the clothes before anyone from the farms or the Nazis arrived, but it didn't stop Peter from being embarrassed about her having stripped him, but his thankfulness soon overcame that.

She now gave him a gruel to drink, and then he slept. Over the next few days, as his wounds healed, he found his neck and shoulders ached badly, but it slowly wore off. Peter found a crucifix hidden in a cupboard by the bed, no doubt because of the persecution of the church. He said a silent thank you, as there was every chance she was Catholic.

He became aware that the deep fear that had been with him ever since he began flying was lifting. Peter wanted to go and see the crash site, but she wouldn't let him. It was too dangerous, the Nazis were emptying the plane of instruments and taking it to bits. He couldn't help the thought going through his mind that with any luck, he would never have to sit in a Lancaster again, and that cheered him. He wondered how those who had escaped were; he hoped they were safe in a POW camp.

One day was Christmas Day, but they couldn't go to Mass. Religion was banned and so they said some prayers and ate a little better than usual. Marta explained there hadn't been a priest since the outbreak of war, he had been taken away and the church desecrated. Peter made a rosary from string, but confession was impossible. So he asked for forgiveness for not going to confession and confessed straight to God.

Marta normally kept her hair under cover, but for that day, she took it down into a long, blonde plait. Peter realised Marta must be about his age, but was too polite to ask. She was slightly shorter than Peter, thickset and strong.

He worried about his family, who now were no doubt grieving for him, so he asked if he could get a letter home through the Polish Underground and she laughed. The chances of any post getting out of Puck were nil. Nor would the Polish Underground risk sending one. While there was hope that the end of the war approached, there would still be much fighting to come.

Every day, he underwent an intensive course in dialect Polish. Marta also made him deepen his voice, no doubt to sound like her husband. He learnt by repeating expressions to reply to the Germans as they might carry out searches. They soon could talk, even if he made mistakes that made her giggle. He found out that she and Piotr had been out poaching rabbits on the night of the crash. The plane had come down so quickly and they had both run in the wrong direction. Piotr had been caught by the burning wing. Peter was truly in his debt.

Peter had never grown a beard before, but was pleased that it now grew out ginger, and Marta approved, Piotr's hair had been a similar hue. Now Peter didn't need any more of the beetroot wash and kept his blonde hair under a hat.

The small house was wooden, dark and very basic, with a tarred roof and tiny windows, with many small rooms, but clean. Peter's small room lay at the back, with a child's bed with a straw mattress and thin blankets, but it was a bed and he was thankful. He wondered if the bed belonged to Piotr when he was a child.

Marta kept Peter indoors, and often she seemed exhausted. In the third week, Peter insisted he learnt to milk, process it, clean the stalls, and all the buckets and urns. Snow now covered everywhere, and ice must be broken on the cows' drinking buckets.

He had never been one for animals, that had been Moira's thing, but he found the gentle beasts calming. His arms ached after the first go at milking and he nearly lost the milk as he stood up, but gradually he got the idea. The red cows were gentle, and their bodies were a source of warmth when he leant on their sides and their gassy, warm breath took the chill off his hands.

As he grew used to manual labour, he became fitter and stronger. It was a hard grind that winter with snow and rain making work difficult. Water froze, hands chapped, backs ached, and they were very often hungry. Peter, shocked out of his public schoolboy complacency, learnt how to work and vowed to himself that in the future, Marta would never have to be so exhausted again.

His back healed rapidly, no doubt because of the cow ointment. It was bitterly cold, and the cows were now inside all the time, so there was much dung to get on the muck heap. One morning, just as they finished milking, bright headlights came along the lane. Marta nearly threw Peter into the bed and told him to act delirious, like in a fever if the Germans came in. She was going to tell them he had cow fever, which people could catch; that should stop visits for a while.

The soldiers popped their heads into the bedroom, but he groaned and writhed in what he hoped seemed a feverish manner, and the door slammed quickly. The soldiers took everything they had, including some potatoes from the kitchen, leaving them with what seemed like precious little.

There were rumours that the Germans were now themselves under pressure, becoming short of food as supply lines failed, but it also meant they had less time for the locals, and there were fewer visits and intimidation. Marta would find the milk churns still where she had delivered them, but empty as town's people siphoned off the contents.

Marta wasn't bothered about the German thefts and showed Peter an earth cellar under the kitchen, with root vegetables and even some bread in boxes. Over the years, some other farmers had returned to supply the invaders, but were not always locals. All were treated as slaves and a lower form of life. Between them, they shared food and formed a network for their own safety.

She hoped that now the allies were starting to win the war after D-Day, the war really might end; she was cautiously optimistic, providing they got there before the Russians. Rumours circulated that the Russian army was on the march. The history of the area told of great enmity between Poland and Russia, let alone now this region was occupied by the Germans. If they were here when the Russians arrived, they would be dead twice, for being Polish and for helping the Germans. If Puck people returned, they would call them collaborators and they would be dead a third time.

APRIL 1945

The Russians were coming, but Marta insisted they waited as long as possible before they fled. The Germans had been in such turmoil for the past few weeks that the farmers were left alone. The chaos of the fighting would hopefully make it easy for them to get away. Peter felt quite a farmer now, and in his easygoing way, almost wished he could stay. He and Marta had become friends, their mutual faith being a strong point as well as their work together.

Marta and Peter hatched a plan to escape, which came about through a chance conversation. They had been discussing how they could get away; it was so far from Warsaw, and the Russians and Germans were reported to be everywhere. The country was in total chaos. They would have to walk to somewhere where the allied troops were, and that might be as far away as France. They really did not know what was going on. There was no radio on the farm, as there was no electricity.

They chatted all the time in their muddled English and Polish, and most of that conversation was about the cows or escaping. Peter would have problems with the English, as he was no longer a British citizen, or even a serving officer. He was

Piotr Nowak.

The farm stood near the coast and the boatyards of Gdynia and Gdansk. There was even a small port of Wladyslawowo that lay to the northwest of them, which had remained a fishing port. Marta had been talking about how tasty some fish would be.

'Piotr used to have a boat up there, and we would go up there and fish of an evening.' She looked sad. But something leapt inside Peter.

'What happened to the boat? What sort was it?'

'He hid it in the reed beds near the harbour. It had one big sail. As you know, he was a bit of a poacher and he would catch fish out of the right season. But it's been years since we were there, and it might have been bombed or stolen, although he was always very careful when we left it for the winter.'

Peter's mind worked overtime. 'But if it's still there, we could use it to sail to Sweden. That's neutral.'

'I've never sailed a boat.'

'I have. I used to be in the Sea Scouts at home and we did lots of night sailing, and I've done navigation courses with the RAF. I can read the stars. I've almost trained for this, except that from the air. Do you have an atlas?'

Marta looked at him as if he was crazy, but came back with an ancient book that fell to pieces in their hands. 'This used to belong to Piotr when he was at school,' she said.

Peter almost snatched it, found the page and, holding it carefully, began reckoning the distances with a piece of paper he marked to nautical miles from the key in the book.

'It's about 190 nautical miles to Karlskrona, the nearest major port. There may even be one closer. There are lots of islands before then. If we ran aground on the coast, we could walk or ask for help. Not that I speak any Swedish.' He lit up and became more excited than Marta had ever seen him.

'But what do we do when we get there? Don't forget you don't have any English papers.'

'If we get to an embassy in a big town, we could simply ring my airbase or my parents. There will be an embassy, I guess, too. I have lots of details I can give that will prove it.'

'And what about me?'

'Well, to start with, we will be a Polish couple, then when we arrive in England, you will be my wife.'

The two stared at each other in astonishment at what Peter had blurted out. He had sensed for a long time that there was something special between them, but never voiced it. He hadn't met many women, he'd been at an all boys' school and in the RAF, a natural fastidiousness stopped him from much of the fun the other airman enjoyed. Marta was so unlike his mother, undemanding, except where the cows were concerned, but with a natural joy about her which crept out sometimes that reminded him of Moira when she was happy.

Marta smiled broadly. 'That is better than Piotr's marriage proposal, he told all of his friends before he asked me.' She took Peter's hand. 'Let's not get to that yet. That's a long way to go, but it can be the goal on our horizon, maybe when we reach Sweden.' Peter nodded and gripped her hand. He had never kissed a girl, so was more than happy to let it wait. At least he didn't have to ask a father, or break it to his mother.

After a couple of days of discussion, planning things, Peter reading the stars, they began packing up, all the time trying to think of all eventualities. They took dry bread, cheeses as that would keep, and it was all they had, anyway. They found old cider bottles that could be resealed for the journey. An old oiled sheet from the barn was fashioned by Marta into a new sail under Peter's guidance using the thick thread, needles, and patches of leather that Piotr's father had used to make the children's shoes. They also packed a small pot of tar for other repairs and old cattle ropes for the mast. Marta fashioned packs for them to carry and repaired their old boots as well as possible. She made small pouches, which would hopefully be waterproof for their documents; they would wear them next to their skin. They tried their packs and found them heavy but bearable. The news of the Russians getting closer meant they would have to go, so one starlit evening, they set out. They didn't tell anyone, having months ago arranged with Ivor next door, that if he found Marta's cows in his field, they had gone. There was no trust anywhere.

They stopped, said a Hail Mary and an Our Father as they stood at the fence, both knowing they would never return. They tramped across the vast, flat fields of the plains, the spring mud clogging their feet. In the dim light, they came to the site of the crash. The silhouette of the plane made Peter shiver. Much had been taken away, but they saw the shape of the Lancaster with the tail up in the air. Peter had thought there might be something he could take as proof, but quickly saw it was useless, it was a burnt-out shell. Together, they prayed over the lost souls and walked on.

By daylight, they reached the woods, and bustled in to hide until the evening. There were plenty of fallen branches, so they hid themselves under a heap and slept the day through. They were fortunate that there were no vagabonds or criminals hiding in the woods.

As the sun sank, they ate a small meal and made their way through the woods to the estuary. They'd taken some risks, as Marta needed some light to find the hiding place.

It seemed that God blessed them as she found the remains of the wooden pier where the boat had been tied up, and there it was. They pulled off the cover. 'Oh no, it's full of water,' Marta couldn't help wailing, then clamped her mouth shut.

'That's not a problem. It means it still holds

water,' Peter grinned. They uncovered it, pulled it up on the bank and set about restoring it, which wasn't easy in the dark. Piotr seemed to have been an expert sailor as the boat had been well caulked, and the only problem was the rotted sail. They struggled with the one made on the farm, but eventually they fitted it and hauled it up and down.

By the time dawn broke, they had packed the yacht and slept in it, covered by the old sail. The next evening, they rowed down the stream that ran through the reeds that now clogged the river to its mouth. By moonrise, they sailed into the open sea.

The sea journey was an anticlimax, with little shipping, and the winds favouring them. Peter saw the stars after the clouds broke. By nightfall the next day, they neared the coast of Sweden.

Then the torpedo boat hit them.

SWEDEN, APRIL, 1945

Lars was on one of his early morning walks along the coast path. Often the tide overnight would bring in something interesting and he needed to check his fish lines by the small, rock built harbour. It was a bright morning, as fresh as the trees in their first flush of spring, which crowded down to the shore. Oh, not again. Something had washed up on the beach. Ever since the war began, bodies had turned up, refugees and servicemen from both sides. But as the war seemed to be ending, he had thought it was all over. It would mean hauling the bodies up, contacting the authorities in Ekenabben and getting them collected. The worse thing was sometimes they weren't in one piece.

He climbed over the rocks. He should check things out, as much as it scared him. There might be a chance they were alive. He found a man and woman in thick peasant clothes. Most unusual; were the Polish running away now too?

The first was a woman. He felt her neck as the doctor had showed him, and, to his surprise, although she was cold, he felt a faint pulse. Likewise with the man. He pulled them both over and up the beach so the sun was on them, and the tide wouldn't seep an extra wave over them. Then Lars ran as fast as he could back to the houses, yelling and shouting for the doctor and things to carry the couple up from the beach.

The villagers took the pair to Johan, the doctor's house, as he had room for them. With the help of his wife, Ingrid, they got them in onto two small beds and shushed the villagers out.

The man had a head wound and deep lacerations that looked like he had been cut with a propeller blade. They bound his head, stitched any wounds that needed it, dressed him in a pair of the doctor's old pyjamas, and put him in bed with a warming pan, leaving him to sleep, nestled in a warm eiderdown. Ingrid, his wife, took his clothes to dry. They put by his bed a pouch he had round his neck. It seemed important.

In the next room, the woman was no less injured by the propeller, but her head was fine. When they were undressing her, they found she was bleeding.

'She's about five months along, Ingrid. Poor girl. We must see what we can do. Get the midwife and see if she has some of those warming pads and if she has any ideas. I guess these two have been through enough. Let's fight for their child.' He sighed, 'I don't think she should be moved at all, so I'll see if I can get some sulphonamides from Karl's surgery in the hospital and we won't tell the authorities just yet.'

The next few days were worrying ones, but

with the antibiotics, both made improvements. It seemed the baby lived, as Johan could hear a heartbeat. It was at that moment when he had the cold trumpet to her stomach that Marta came around. They all laughed later, and said it must have been Johan's chilly hands as well as the trumpet.

She jumped away from him in fear. Johan recognised her words as Polish and used the little he had to calm her. But it seemed to make her worse when he told her the baby was ok. She coiled into a ball and began howling. Did she want to lose the baby? Eventually, she calmed through Ingrid's clucking and soothing.

'Are there any Polish refugees still in the town?' He asked Ingrid.

'Not that I know of, but the Mayor will, I'll call him.' She bustled off, and Johan went to check on the man. He seemed to be sleeping soundly and yet muttering. Johan caught some words. This was even more bewildering; he was talking to his mother in English.

Johan sat down on a chair and puzzled. Perhaps the only thing to do was to check the pouches they both carried. When he opened them, he only found their German identifications, which said they were both Polish. What could he do but wait until Piotr came round?

It took several more days before he did, and at first Peter didn't realise he was being spoken to in English and answered the questions, telling of their flight from near Puck and being run over by the torpedo boat, but not much more.

'So why is an Englishman carrying the ID of a Polish man?' It was at that point that it all dawned on Peter and he turned paler than before.

'I'm not telling you anymore until I know exactly where I am, when it is, and why you can speak to me in English.'

Johan explained he was safe in Sweden, near the town of Ekenabben. That seemed to satisfy Peter momentarily. The tall, bespectacled doctor and his short, blonde wife had many years with difficult patients and knew how to deal with them with patience and love.

'Your wife and the baby are doing well, but she will have to stay in bed or be very careful until the birth in September.'

'The what?' Peter tried very hard to keep his reserve, but it wasn't easy after such a shock. It made him realise he must tell the entire story, which he did, and when he finished he made it clear, stating firmly, 'We do plan to get married, but this child isn't mine. It must be Piotr's.'

'If you are aircrew, we must contact the embassy in Stockholm and get your family informed,' Johan said. Peter was surprised at how hesitant he felt about that. He needed time to think. 'Could we not rush into anything? I need to see Marta and talk things through.'

'But of course. Now, I have a very elderly old bath-chair. Would you like to go in it to see her?'

Johan was touched by the tenderness when the two saw each other. They sat there talking in Polish, so he left them in privacy. This was all most extraordinary.

'So he told you about the baby?' asked Marta.

'Naturally, why didn't you tell me?'

'You won't believe me, but I wasn't sure. I put it down to being so thin and the hard things we were going through. Piotr would have loved a son.' She burst into tears. It was the first time she had ever showed any emotion about her husband and it stunned the pair of them.

'Will you plan to go to England now?' She seemed to have forgotten his pledge.

'No, I said I will have you as a wife, but we both need to heal, and the baby born. Then we'll get married and make our way back.' He found a sudden strength. 'I am in debt to Piotr. It will be an honour to raise his child. Marta, it's all over. We're safe. There's no hurry. I might write and tell my family, but I will stay here with you. I don't want to get caught up in the war again.'

'But if it's not over, surely you should fly again?'

'We can wait a while. After all, we are injured.' Peter couldn't even face the thought of flying again. Anything that would put off that eventuality was good.

That seemed to set things for the next few weeks. Both of them were weak, and the effects of their injuries made their recovery slow. Johan and

Ingrid became their friends and moved them into bedrooms in their summer house in the garden, as Marta needed to avoid any strenuous actions. She was still having occasional spottings of blood.

The villagers took them to heart and were in and out, practising their Polish. They had been asked not to tell the town community in case the authorities stepped in, although Sweden wasn't interested in refugees, as most were preparing to leave or transiting home. Peter, Marta, and Johan had also agreed to keep Peter's identity secret until the right time.

Peter must tell his family. It flew round and round in his mind about what he should do. A phone call would cause confusion and a riot, especially as it wouldn't be coming through the RAF. A letter the same. Contacting the RAF might have military police coming for him, although Johan, when asked, said he would sign anything to confirm that Peter had been unfit to travel because of his injuries.

The weeks sped on, and the abundant spring was a joy. Then came the day in May when Johan came pounding down the garden. 'It's over, it's over. There is peace in Europe, my friends. You are forever safe.'

The news brought a joy to the pair, and Peter knew he must write at least. He would tell them some of the truth. There would be a full explanation when he got back, especially when he turned up with a wife and child. He decided to say that he had been recovering from injuries, or maybe on some special operation, top secret, but then, they would be unable not to broadcast it everywhere. The British authorities would hear and want to interrogate him. He knew that was protocol, but not what it would entail. How could he tell them without his mother organising an ambulance to collect him? She would tell all of Winchester. Perhaps he should just tell Father, but that would be unfair, too. So he prevaricated, often reaching to write and then putting the paper down, and enjoyed the Swedish spring swinging into summer.

Marta was happy too and bloomed with the good food and pregnancy. Peter never seemed to put on weight, but he grew a little and filled out. It had long worried him they were being fed and looked after for nothing, and that he owed the villagers a great deal. They brought both of them clothes, boots, baby clothes, and all sorts of herbal remedies. Peter and Marta had nothing to repay them with, so Peter tried to make himself useful to anyone in the village.

The village was situated a hundred metres from the coast; so the villagers made their living with fishing. The brackish waters of the Baltic sea grew large fresh-water fish as well as cod, herring and sprats. These were caught and sold in the town. Each house had a garden, and one couple even had a house cow, although the wooded island didn't have much grazing on that side. Peter learnt to garden and to fish, even going out with some boats, and afterwards net mending. His days were always full. Marta wasn't left alone either. The children came after school to the summerhouse, playing and trying to teach her Swedish. Their mothers taught Marta how to knit and mend, so there was always a pile of socks. She found familiar things to do too, such as storing as helping with preparing fish for smoking.

On the summer solstice in June, the villagers raised a maypole on the green with much merriment. Marta, being allowed to join in, was pushed along in the old bath-chair. Everyone drank brännvin or vodka. It was an idyllic time, so long as Peter could squash his guilt about home.

However, one thing bothered the pair of them. Both Catholics they had landed in a Lutheran country, there were no Catholic churches or priests. They both felt the need to make confession and wanted to have the sacrament. They took this to Johan, who smiled and told them to leave it to him.

One evening, they were sitting in the garden as it grew cooler, when a tall, rather unkempt man strode into the garden, where they were sitting. He was a shock, scruffily dressed with ragged, long, greying hair. Instinctively, Marta and Peter drew together.

'Hey, people, be not afraid. I am Tadek and Johan asked me to come and talk to you.'

He shook their hands and drew himself up a

chair before they could speak. He talked in Polish, so Marta plucked up the courage to ask him where he came from.

'Lithuania, so we are cousins. Now Johan has said you are Catholics, and you are missing your church. I did too, until I came here, a refugee like yourselves. I was a priest, but I am now a member of the local Lutheran church. Isn't that astonishing?' He continued, almost without drawing breath. 'I understand you wish to make your confessions, and that I can do. The church has never officially traced me or taken my priesthood away. But there are many truths and lies in the church, and I must tell you these first.'

He put his head on the side and waited for their nods.

'When did you last read your Bibles? A long time, I expect. Do you know it never tells you to confess to a man, but to God himself? Who, when you are truly repentant, has already forgiven you? It will soon be two thousand years since Jesus died, so logically, he died for all sin, past, present and future. All your sins are already forgiven.' He reached into his pockets, and brought out two Bibles, one in English, one in Polish.

'Then we must talk about the communion, it's not an actual body. No, it's deeply, beautifully symbolic, which is no less mystical. Why do you go to Maria? She was only a woman, a blessed one, just go straight to Jesus. He will heal, forgive, and love you. He did it all on the cross. Receive in faith what he did for you, all healing and goodness.'

The man was a steamroller. Peter and Marta looked at each other, both feeling that many things they believed in were being pulled from under their feet.

'I can see it's a lot to take in. Let me pray for you. Dear Father, thank you for bringing Peter and Marta to safety. We lift up to you their baby and ask for its safe arrival. That they will soon be able to travel home and begin a new life as a family. Holy Spirit, please open their hearts and minds as they read your word and know your truth. Amen.'

What could they say but Amen?

Now Tadek had said all he wanted to, he calmed a little, and the chat became more general. They sensed the love and kindness flowing from him. The skies were deepening into night and Tadek took his leave, promising to return in a few days and see what they wanted to do.

Peter looked at Marta. 'You know, I've been confessing directly to God all the time, and hoping that it didn't make him angry with me. Now I feel at peace, that it was fine with him. It goes against all that I've been taught in school, but it's a little like some sort of weight has lifted.'

Marta burst out laughing. 'I've been doing the same thing. It's such a habit going to confession that I knew I was bottling up my sins and had to let them out. Maybe we don't need to have him hear our confession, but I really would like communion.'

The two took the proffered Bibles, and over the next few days, read them. When Tadek returned, they had many questions for him as they disregarded the things that had tied them in the past and looked afresh at their faith. Peter felt only one reservation. What would his mother say to this? His father, a Protestant, would just smile and say, 'there's always two sides to a coin.' However, taking communion again was a boost and a joy as they felt healing from the injuries of war, grief, and hurt. It was as if they were lifting from them.

Tadek was with them the night in early September when Marta's pains began. He whisked Peter away to one of the houses in the village, and they plied him gently with vodka as the hours passed.

At about midnight came a knock at the door. It was Ingrid. 'Peter, you must come. All is not going well. We must take her to the hospital.'

She wouldn't give details, but when he got to Marta, he took her hand and did the best to be of comfort. An ambulance arrived, then in the hospital, she was rushed away. Tadek and Peter were very good at pacing by the time a nurse came in with a bundle in her arms.

'Which of you is Piotr?' Peter stepped forward, and took the bundle and peered into a pink, squeezed up face that reminded him of Winston Churchill.

'This is your daughter. Mother is sleeping after the caesarean operation. Do you have a name for her?'

'Yes. Petra Maria. Look Tadek, she's perfect.'

It didn't matter that this wasn't his own child, she was his firstborn. Together, he and Tadek prayed for child and mother, then gave her back.

1946

Marta took a long time to recover from the operation. There were complications, and she even needed to make some trips back to the hospital for further treatment. Peter and Marta enjoyed the Christmas celebrations, and the novelty of snow they didn't have to work in, but in early March, they were both determined it was time to go. It was a wrench to leave the village, but they could always write, and maybe come for a holiday.

Tadek looked so sad to see them go, he would miss his sparring partners as they often argued and laughed about their faith. In their long conversations, he never demanded they agree, just encouraged them to think and pray and test what they thought with what the Bible said. He sometimes won the arguments, and sometimes he didn't, but as they discussed things with love, it never became a problem. He never spoke of what had happened in Lithuania, and they left him alone on that. Peter and Marta even attended the local chapel with him occasionally, and while the language was still a problem, the spirit was there, and the services filled them with joy. They didn't miss the bells and incense.

One day, shortly before they left, the pastor

of the church and Tadek baptised Petra, and married Peter and Marta. They didn't dress up or make a party of it; it just felt right to do this in the eyes of God with people they loved and trusted. Peter had already warned Marta about his mother's strict Catholicism.

The entire village had clubbed together, and they found themselves with a suitcase of clothes for them and baby. Plus, most of all, money that would pay for their train to Stockholm. They had already made an appointment at the British embassy and were quite worried about how it would go.

If he could prove he was Peter Croft, they would get married legally at the town hall and, hopefully Marta would then have no problem travelling with Peter. He still worried he might be arrested, but he had the attestation from Johan about his injuries; he hoped that would do.

When they reached the embassy, the first reaction of the rather straight-faced young man at the desk was disbelief. He marched the three into another office, where they had to go through the entire story several times, showing their IDs. They then marched again into a palatial office, and in strode the ambassador, who with a huge grin pumped Peter's hand up and down, and welcomed him home.

The process kicked in with more interviews and form filling. The major rush of POWs had been the previous year when Operation Exodus brought thousands home. But prisoners were still returning; Peter and Marta weren't alone. The Embassy gave them a small room until such time as they could fly back to London. All this took a month or so until Peter finally got a passport and Marta documentation so she could leave Sweden. The only person who had no problem was Petra, being a Swedish national. All had been arranged and Peter, Marta with Petra took themselves to the town hall and got married officially one quiet afternoon.

They arrived in London on a bright April morning and had to go to the Air Ministry at Whitehall for Peter's interrogation. This proved far less scary than expected, and he gave them much information about what the Germans had been up to in Puck. Marta had a lot to tell them too, which could be used in war crimes trials. The Russians now controlled Poland, and it seemed there was little peace in that region yet. Peter was thrilled to find two of his crew had also made it home, only a few weeks before him. They had taken just as long as he had, so he looked forward to meeting them. However, 106 Squadron had been disbanded in February, so that would be difficult, but he realised he had plenty of time. The officials also told Peter there would be a more than an acceptable amount of back pay in his account. Once the departments were convinced he wasn't dead, he would be demobbed.

It was also going to take a mountain of

bureaucracy to change the name on the grave in Puck, or even get it moved to a local graveyard, not a commonwealth one. Peter was glad that wouldn't be his headache.

He just wanted to be home with the family and show them his own. He had asked that no telegram be sent; he wanted to arrive, see the pandemonium himself, and share their joy with them. Peter itched to see how the shop was, the new home, what his sister was up to, take up the reins of family life and move on as if the war had never taken place. Quite what his mother would do when he arrived with a wife and child, and some ideas that would go against her deeply ingrained religion would be interesting.

Finally, after many months, came the time to go home. They had a generous amount of money for the tickets, and maybe they would even take a taxi from the station. Peter guessed that his family would have all moved to Morton House the previous year, but knew any taxi driver would know where his father lived. On the train to Winchester, he read how the Grand National had been run for the first time since the outbreak of war. Things were getting back to normal.

END

SUNDAY 7TH APRIL 1946

Moira returned from the pub, and after a very nice goodnight kiss from Monty, was in a joyful frame of mind. The house was silent, apart from voices coming from the sitting room. She needed to sort her mother out for once and for all. She let the anger rise and prepared for battle when she opened the door.

To her surprise, her parents had visitors, and Moira was backing out when her mother saw her. It was most strange; she was smiling and crying at the same time. 'Moira, dear, look who's here.' So she did, taking in a plump woman with blonde hair holding a small baby. The pair hadn't noticed her arrival, being deep in discussion with Father. Oddly dressed in shabby clothes, they reminded her of the pictures she had seen of refugees. What were they doing here? Another charity case for Father? She looked at the man, and looked, and looked as he returned her stare, a smile grew on his face.

'Peter!' Moira rushed in and, throwing down all her prepared battle and family reticence, hugged him. The tumult of emotions overwhelmed her. She stood back to look at him again. Then they were all crying, even Father. Peter was taller, broader, and somehow much older, but it was him. Miracles happened, and so Moira, for a fleeting moment, actually said a thank you to God.

Over the next couple of hours, Peter told the full story of the air crash and their escape from Poland. Moira now had a sister in law, and was an aunt; it was an awful lot to take in. Her mother didn't even raise an eyebrow when it became clear that Petra wasn't Peter's daughter. If Peter said he was the father, and Marta his wife, in their joy, she would accept it too.

Gill brought in sandwiches, and one of the bottles of champagne left over from the party. Mother seemed transformed, she smiled all the time, a new occurrence. Eventually, the yawns prevailed, and all knew they must go to bed. They would all meet again in the morning, no more partings. Peter and Marta had the best bedroom, but baby Petra had to go into a drawer until a cot could be bought.

Late next morning, Moira was awoken by a tap on the door, which the dogs rushed to answer. Peter came in and plonked himself on her bed like when they were children and as if he'd never been away.

'So, how are things with you? Mother says you're really into the racing. I saw the National ran again. Good for you getting into something, and not sitting at home. How was it while I was thought missing? There really was no way to get a message home. You can't believe what brutality we saw when we were delivering milk. The Germans were inhuman. We were blessed to get away during the chaos at the end.'

'Yes, we must hate the Germans forever, so it doesn't happen again,' Moira jumped in.

'No, don't let the hate eat you, Moira.' His voice was stern. 'We mustn't forget, but we have to rebuild the world so there is no repetition of all this hatred and killing. Love is the way forward, being constructive, not descending to their levels. Let it go.' He'd never rebuked her like that before, even in their arguments. Something began melting inside of her as she considered what he had said.

'I went to Mass with Mother this morning. It wasn't easy.' Moira, preparing to groan, looked up with interest. 'During our stay in Sweden, I came across a lot of new ideas about God. It doesn't mean I'll leave the church. It's too ingrained, too familiar and comforting. But there is a lot wrong with the thinking in there.'

'I've been saying that and getting slapped down for it for a long time,' Moira almost laughed. 'We are going to have an interesting time with Mother over this. Does that mean you're staying, not going back to Poland?'

'Maybe in the far future, when things are settled. But right now, my dream is to make a home for my family and run the business. It's all I ever wanted.'

'And Father, he was training me with a lot of things, but horses are really what I want to build my life around.'

'No reason why you can't do both, is there? It's not as if you will be in charge of the shop, it will be a real family business,' Peter grinned broadly.

'You've been thinking and planning this for a long time!' Moira realised she had completely forgotten about the family business in all her discussions with Monty.

'Oh, yes. Marta is happy to be safe, and she's already looking at the cows next door. I think she will do a lot of gardening and maybe we'll have a small farm. Everything has a new beautiful promise, that we can make it as we want. Aren't we lucky, so fortunate to be given a new chance when so many are grieving? We must share this good fortune too, possibly help other families who are wounded.'

'So you're going to be Saint Peter now, are you?' laughed Moira with some of her former vivacity. 'Mother will be so pleased.'

'No, she'll have to be kept firmly under control.'

'Mother?'

'She's been bitter, grieving for a long time, we mustn't let her slip back into her old ways,' Peter said firmly.

'She's always been rotten to me. Do you know what she did to Puck, and what she said to Monty?'

'She mentioned some things on the way back this morning. You two need to have a chat.'

'I'm not going to be her lapdog. She's never even forgiven me for being born.'

'I know, Moira, and I owe you an explanation.'

To Moira's shock, her mother stood at the door, heavens knows how long she had been there. She came in and shoved Nimbus off the chair, but with more affection that ever before.

'As you know, I had two sisters, and as the eldest, I was always left looking after them when mother worked. Fetch them from school, cook for them. I hated it. That is why I left Cardiff as soon as I could to work for the post office in London. I was stuck with their childishness and nothing left for me. I felt like an unpaid servant.'

'Shouldn't you be saying this to Nan, not me?' Moira asked.

'I have done, now, let me finish,' she said with her former asperity. 'Then Bridget committed suicide, and I was overwhelmed with guilt and couldn't find a way to repent of it.'

'So that's why Nan won't talk about Henry's mum. Go on,' said Moira.

'When I got married, I didn't want any girls of my own, and I sort of let it fester in me, not taking it to confession. I'm sorry I sent you to school younger than Peter. I do want you as my daughter. I'm sorry I put Puck down, it was spite. I tried to warn Monty off in my determination to get you out of the house and into a Catholic family which would put you under control.'

'Like Cecil?'

Her mother turned red. That was something new.

'Moira, I'm sorry. The Lord has brought my son back to me, and I wasn't deserving of that. I need to make amends and live the life that will be pleasing in His sight. I can't say better than that, can I? Please forgive me, Moira?'

What could she do but give a nod? Inside her, Moira felt something frozen melting inside her, even though she knew there was more to this, it would take time to understand each other and not get back into their old habits.

Father burst in with a huge grin on his face. 'Now, everyone, as we are all friends again, I think there has to be a major shopping trip to Winchester. Grandmother, aunt, son, wife and granddaughter. I want to parade you in my town and tell the world.' Everyone agreed and left Moira to get dressed. Father slipped her a wink and the most joyous smile she'd ever seen. Moira had a sudden realisation of how tired and sad he had been looking, now that he looked happy again. She knew there would still be battles with her mother, especially when they heard what she and Monty were planning with the stables and her part in them.

Peter was the last to leave the room, and he turned to her. 'I say, you didn't tell the folks about my pranged car, did you?'

EPILOGUE

Fact is stranger than fiction, but if you enjoyed the tale, and want to remember the Crofts in their happiness, you may want to skip this and go straight to the gallery.

So now the tale is done, with a happy ending, but life isn't like that, really. A lot of this tale is true. I've put together all that was said over the years, and imagined the background to events.

Moira's life was far more complicated than this story, and she had no real happy ending, all of which you can read in my memoirs, for I am her daughter. Moira and her mother never reconciled, fighting until the end. I think it was also an act of rebellion by my mother to marry my father. He was not only not a Catholic, but he was also divorced. If you wish to read the whole story of my family, you can find them in my 'God, horses and love memoirs.' which are also available on Amazon.

The letters are all authentic. I've typed them exactly as they were written, but dates have been changed to fit the narrative. Things like the fate of Peter's car, I've made up. I've changed Moira's age to fit my timeline. She was 16 in 1944. Oh, I have so many questions I want to ask her, to get more detail and straighten out some details I can't work out which niggle me, but she is long gone.

The family ran Crofts and Sons in Winchester until the late sixties. It went bust because of under capitalisation. I always thought I would spend my life running the shop. It was a great disappointment when it closed.

My grandfather was an entrepreneur, and had fingers in many pies, owning a lot of properties in Winchester, which I discovered while researching this book. He was a bad photographer and a Scout, being on the first Scout Camp on Brownsea Island with Baden Powell. I so wish I could have met him. Moira said he would have spoilt me rotten.

My grandmother was a difficult woman, but it was her doggedness that kept the hunt for Peter going until there really was no other ending. And she did have Puck put down. It was her ill health after two operations that closed the club down in 1950.

I've told you most of this from things Moira told me, and in 1980, she wrote me an account of the country club. To me it seemed a childhood dream come true, horses, fun and games and stables outside the bedroom window. Morton House later became an Old People's home, but now is gone, buried under a housing estate. Tommy's stables have also vanished, but one block that remains has been converted into a house.

Tommy Rayson trained Lovely Cottage. His

son, Monty, was an up-and-coming jockey, but sadly, he died of suspected food poisoning on his honeymoon before 1945. I changed this, so I could write Moira her dream ending.

Cottage's real jockey, Captain Bobby Petre, was a friend of Tommy's. He really did oversleep and had to rush to get to the race. I've used a lot of his personal account in Monty's telling of the race. Bobby's story in the following years might make another book!

Maybe there was a party for Cottage's return home, we'll never know! He didn't run in the 1947 Grand National due to injury. In 1948, he was only placed. Before retiring to the Murrays home, where he was buried when he died, he spent time in the summers being taken around village fetes as a star attraction.

Amber was very much as she was in my story. She also bolted through Kings Worthy with the governess cart. When they tried to get her to pull the mower and cut the grass at Morton House, she kicked the boots off, which were needed to protect the grass, and took off again. My mother was really fond of her.

Cecil existed, Gran tried to marry Moira off to him. The galloping down hills and bolting racehorse in Leatherhead were true as well as her broken thumb.

The phone call by Rudy was recorded by Moira, which she said was, 'ironic.' Certainly an understatement. The raid took place over Gdynia, and Peter never came home. He's buried in a Commonwealth grave in Poland. I've even found the name of the pilot who claimed the kill. Peter noticing the time of 22.12, was the actual time his plane was shot down, as recorded by the German pilot. Moira always wanted to visit Peter's grave, but never made it. I think she lost courage each time the opportunity arose. She treasured the photos sent to her.

As I finish writing this book in November 2022, it's shortly before Remembrance Sunday. I have Peter's medals and will wear them for him at the ceremony, as no one has recognised his memory in this way, they were still in the original box. I do it for all those who gave their lives in any war, but also for Peter, who I feel I have come to know as I've read about him, seen his log book and war record, and the photos the family has kept.

GALLERY

I have done my best with the photos to make them as clear as possible!

The Croft Family before the war. Peter, Mother (Mary Ann), Father (Harold), Moira.

Morton House

A view of the garden where many parties took place.

Ready for a tennis party?

Mother's sitting room, look closely at the pictures on the wall.

The main hall

One of the parties, I guess these steps were around the other side of the house. Cecil is sitting on the right pillar with Moira beside him. Fifi is in the middle of the steps left of the large woman in a white top.

Mother, Tommy Rayson and Stan from next door

Moira Nora Croft
I'm sure Mother made her have this photo taken!

Moira on the lawn with broken thumb,
Puck, Raoul in a heap and Nimbus.

Moira and the irrepressible Amber

Moira off to the races with one of the owners, this one made me giggle!

Peter Frederick Croft

I think he must have had a sense of humour, in many of the photos, he's always the one sitting differently to the others. Maybe also a sense of being apart as in his RAF photos he's often standing apart from the groups.

Peter at school

Peter and his crew of Lancaster
bomber NN726, 106 Squadron

From Left to right
F/O B. F. Croft - Air Bomber (Peter)
F/Lt M. S. F. Pritchard - Captain (Roby)
Sgt. S. Robinson - W/operator (Ted, R)
Sgt. E. W. Skipper - Flt Engineer (Pilot)
Sgt. F. J. Turkentine - Navigator (Basil)
Sgt. R. Egglestone - M/Upr Gunner (Ron)
Sgt. H. Ainley - Rear Gunner (Rusty

I'm guessing on this one!
Peter, Basil,Skipper, Rusty, Roby, Ron, Ted.

Lovely Cottage himself!

Finally, my favourite picture on Moira, my Mum in her fifties, with her first grandson, Peter.

DEAR READER, THANK YOU!

I hope you have enjoyed In Plain Sight!

Please leave a review on Amazon. It means so much to indie authors!

There are many ways to catch up with my books. My blog, Anna's Horse Books, acts like a mailing list. Once a month will come books, interviews, special offers, and much more. There is also an Advent Calendar which will give you loads of ideas for Christmas horse book gifts. On the Homepage, just click on follow by email at the foot of the page, or click on the follow widget if you are on Wordpress.

https://booksbyanna619772285.wordpress.com/

You can also join me in my Facebook group for horse book readers. Horse Books for Grown Ups.

https://www.facebook.com/groups/1979909005465261

You can find my Author page on Facebook

https://www.facebook.com/horsesandogs

Twitter: Anna Rashbrook@AnnaRashbrook

BIBLIOGRAPHY

'Caught napping.' *Southern Evening Echo* 4th April 1986; author unknown

Dent, Captain C. H. Second Fiddle, son of Viola Hutchinson & Co London (1951)

Dent, Captain C. H. The Copper Horse: story of a Steeplechasing Horse from his point of view Hutchinson & Co London (1948)

Dent, Captain C. H. Head High, Hands Low - A Story of Horses, Ponies and Riders Hutchinson & Co London (1949)

Dent, Captain C H. The Horse has four legs. Dublin (1944)

Hogg Gemma, Stable Lass: Tales from a Yorkshire Stable Yard PanMacmillan (2018)

Heathcote, Violet M Fiander's horses, Oxford University Press (1953

Theo Boten, Nachtjagd, Combat Archive 1944, Part 5, Red Kite Books (2021)

Price, David The Crew: the Story of a Lancaster Bomber Crew (2020)

Winsor, Kathleen Forever Amber Macmillan (1944)

Wells H. G., The Wheels of Chance J M Dent (1896)

Green Reg, The History of the Grand National, A Race apart Teach yourself paperback (1993)

TV

Timeline. The History of the Lancaster bomber.

FILM

The Rainbow Jacket, Ealing studios, 1954

WEBSITES

The jockey club.co.uk

Horse Racing: Aintree; Grandnationalanorak2.com

www.britishlegion.org.uk/stories/being-a-bomb-aimer

www.iwm.org.uk/history/whos-who-in-an-raf-bomber-crew

tangmere-museum.org

Internationalbcc.co.uk

bombergateway.co.uk

everycare.co.uk/miraculous escapes, Reg Barker

metheringhamairfield.co.uk

Printed in Great Britain
by Amazon

12701097R00148